COLOR

for the Decorative Painter

COLOR

for the Decorative Painter

~ Sandra Aubuchon, CDA ~

NORTH LIGHT BOOKS

CINCINNATI, OHIO

~ www.nlbooks.com ~

About the Author

Sandy Aubuchon is an internationally known artist, author and teacher. She has been painting for over thirty years and has published more than forty painting books. In addition to teaching at conventions and demonstrating at trade shows in the United States, she travels the world teaching classes and studying folk art painting styles. She then adapts these native painting styles to projects for the American painter.

Color for the Decorative Painter. Copyright (c) 2001 by Sandra Aubuchon. Manufactured in China. All rights reserved. The patterns and drawings in this book are for the personal use of the decorative painter. By permission of the author and publisher, they may be either hand-traced or photocopied to make single copies, but under no circumstances may they be resold or republished. It is permissible for the purchaser to paint the designs contained herein and sell them at fairs, bazaars and craft shows. No other part of this book may be reproduced in any form or by any electronic or mechanical means including information storage and retrieval systems without permission in writing from the publisher, except by a reviewer, who may quote brief passages in a review. Published by North Light Books, an imprint of F&W Publications, Inc., 1507 Dana Avenue, Cincinnati, Ohio 45207. (800) 289-0963. First edition.

Other fine North Light Books are available from your local bookstore, art supply store or direct from the publisher.

05 04 03 02 01   5 4 3 2

Library of Congress Cataloging-in-Publication Data

Aubuchon, Sandy.
    Color for the decorative painter / by Sandra Aubuchon.– 1st ed.
        p. cm.
    Includes index.
    ISBN 1-58180-048-7 (pbk. : alk. paper)
    1. Painting–Technique. 2. Decoration and ornament. 3. Color in art. I. Title.

TT385 .A93 2001
745.7'23–dc21   00-048029

Editor: Christine Doyle
Production Coordinator: Kristen D. Heller
Designer: Andrea Short
Layout Artist: Melissa Wilson
Photographers: Christine Polomsky and Al Parrish

Dedication

This book is dedicated to the Society of Decorative Painters. The Society is a U.S. organization that consists of chapters of painters all over the world. They all work and teach together to spread the art and fun of decorative painting.

Acknowledgments

I want to thank the Society of Decorative Painters for the chance to teach decorative painting around the world. Without this organization, I would never have had this opportunity.

I would also like to thank the following for their generous contributions to this book:

EAGLE BRUSH
431 Commerce Park Dr., Ste. 100
Marietta, GA 30060
800-832-4532

HOUSTON ART FRAME
distributor of Athena Grey Palette
10770 Moss Ridge Road
Houston, TX 77043-1175
800-272-3804
www.houstonart.com

BRUSHWORKS
P. O. Box 1467
Moreno Valley, CA 92556
909-653-3780

CATALINA COTTAGE
125 N. Aspen, Unit 5
Azusa, CA 91702
Orders only: 800-787-6685
626-969-4001

DESIGNS BY BENTWOOD
170 Big Star Dr.
Thomasville, GA 31792
912-226-1223

VIKING WOODCRAFTS, INC.
1317 8th St. S.E.
Waseca, MN 56093
800-328-0116
www.vikingwoodcrafts.com

WALNUT HOLLOW
1409 State Road 23
Dodgeville, WI 53533
Orders only: 800-950-5101

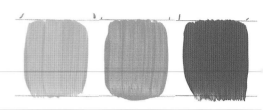

INTRODUCTION, 9

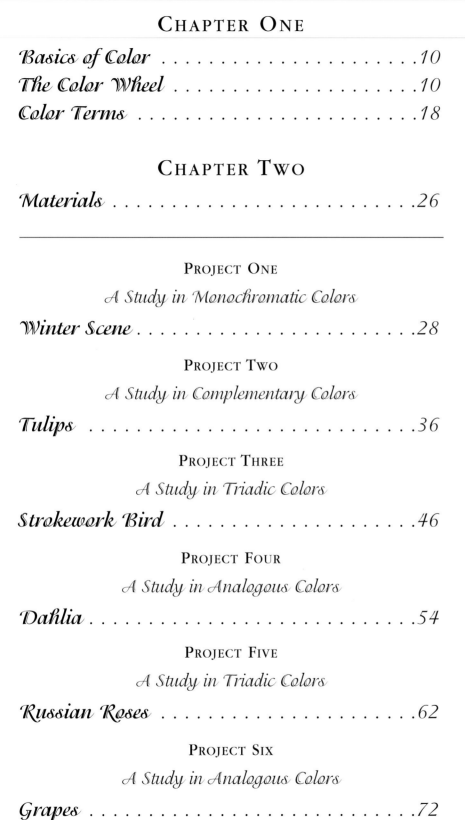

Introduction

WITHOUT COLOR, LIFE would be so dull. Color is everywhere, every day of our lives. Everything we see—in our homes, in our workplace, anywhere we go—brings color into our lives. Outside colors help to signal the changes in the seasons—from the pink and green of spring and the yellow and blue of summer to the orange and brown of autumn and the red and black of winter. Color can make us happy, sad, excited or very solemn. Its influence can be felt in every aspect of our lives.

Color is important, of course, to the decorative painter as well. Knowledge of color will make decorative painting so much easier. You will be able to understand why colors are placed in certain areas of a painting, how colors work together and what effect color combinations have on the people who see your work. With the basics of color, you will be able to take the struggle out of painting and enjoy the process even more.

Over the years color has somehow acquired a reputation for being very difficult to understand. And often, color instruction does present too much information too quickly. When I was a beginning artist, I was overwhelmed by color, but nothing I could find related to a beginner. This is the book I wish I'd had those many years ago—color explained and illustrated in a way everyone can understand. With this book you will learn to walk before you run!

In it, you will learn to take color apart and then put it back together one piece at a time. By first learning about the colors in the color wheel, you will establish a firm base for your new understanding of color. Then, you will learn about the relationships of the colors on the color wheel and what effects combinations of these colors will produce. A section on color terms will introduce you to more aspects of color that will impact your painting—things like temperature, intensity and contrast. Finally, I will give you the opportunity to put your knowledge to use with projects that illustrate the different color combinations and concepts discussed in the beginning chapter.

Everyone needs a place to start. I hope this book will be a starting place for the beginning artist (and the more advanced) to better understand color. Just give yourself a chance to learn about color and develop your painting talents. You will be surprised how much you can do with just a little practice.

I know your time is valuable. Invest your time in painting. And enjoy!

CHAPTER ONE

The Basics of Color

THE COLOR WHEEL

Many of us painters have been in a situation where we want to paint a piece using a certain color, but just aren't sure what other colors to use with it. Maybe you end up guessing at which colors to use, with mixed results, or perhaps you give up altogether. Those of us without a god-given eye for color can turn to the color wheel in this situation for a variety of color suggestions.

The color wheel consists of twelve basic colors placed in specific spots in a circle. The relationship between these colors determines whether colors will look good together and what the effect of the combination will be. First, let's look at the colors in the color wheel, how they are mixed and where they are placed. Then I'll discuss the different relationships between these colors.

Colors in the Color Wheel

PRIMARY COLORS

The basis for the color wheel is the three primary colors: red, yellow and blue. The pure forms of these colors cannot be achieved by mixing other colors. It is the combinations of these colors that make up all the other colors on the color wheel. The acrylic paint companies have different names for these colors. DecoArt calls them Primary Red, Primary Blue and Primary Yellow. Check the conversion chart in the back of this book for the name used by your favorite paint company.

❧ *The three primary colors are spaced at an equal distance apart on the color wheel, usually with yellow at the top.*

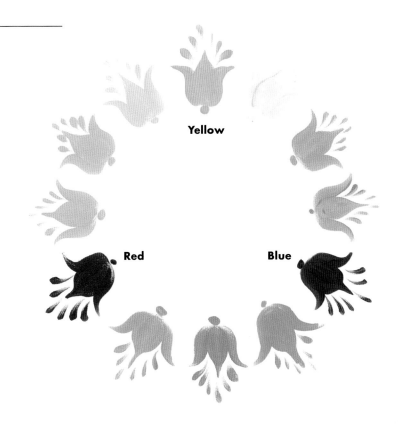

SECONDARY COLORS

Mixing any two of the primary colors will create the three secondary colors on the color wheel. When making these colors, you're not necessarily mixing equal parts, but just enough to achieve the color you feel is between the two primary colors.

❧ *Secondary colors are placed between the two primary colors that were mixed to create them.*

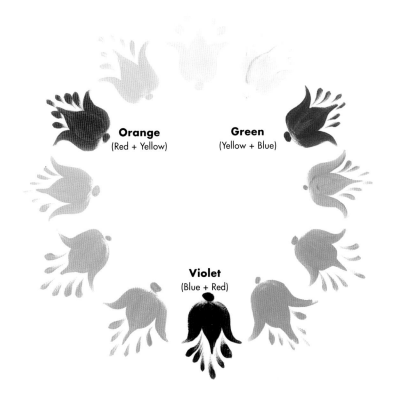

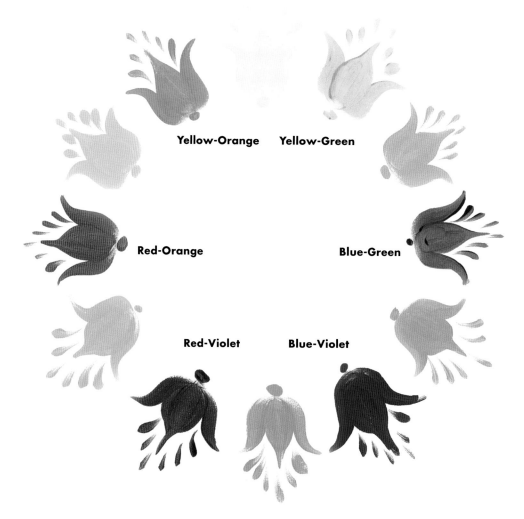

Yellow-Orange   Yellow-Green

Red-Orange   Blue-Green

Red-Violet   Blue-Violet

INTERMEDIATE OR TERTIARY COLORS

The six tertiary colors are made by mixing a primary color with the secondary color next to it on the color wheel. Again, these are not necessarily equal portions, but just enough to make a color you feel falls in-between the two you are mixing. When naming these colors, always say the primary color name first.

❧ *The tertiary colors are placed between the primary and secondary colors mixed to create them.*

Color Combinations

Understanding the color wheel itself is the first step. Now let's look at how it can be used to help you determine color combinations when painting. The following are five "formulas" for understanding the color wheel, each using a different combination of colors. You need to learn to walk before you can run, so let's start with the combination using the fewest number of colors, just one, and move to the combination that would allow you to use the full spectrum of colors.

MONOCHROMATIC COLORS

This formula is the easiest because it uses just one color from the color wheel—plus black and white. The effect will be very soft and subtle. Use this color combination when you want to paint a piece that adds interest to a room but isn't wild or overpowering. It's great for accent pieces where a bit of color is all that's needed.

By mixing the one color, in this case blue, with varying amounts of black and white, you can use a wide variety of values in your painting.

❧ I painted this piece for my husband's den. The room is dark, with a leather desk and orange plaid cushions on the furniture. I wanted to paint something to sit on the desk and add a little color. I chose to use blue, the complement of orange (see page 15), in this subdued color combination because I think it works well in a man's room. This project begins on page 28.

ANALOGOUS COLORS

Analogous colors are three to five colors that lie side by side on the color wheel. Colors that touch each other on the color wheel will be similar because the same colors are used to make each. For example, with the analogous colors of yellow, yellow-orange, and orange, yellow was used to make orange, and both yellow and orange make up yellow-orange. Since the colors are quite similar, the effect of using analogous colors will be subtle. Like the monochromatic scheme, this color combination works well for accent pieces that will add color to a room without attracting a lot of attention.

For analogous, and all of the combinations that use multiple colors, you can create more colors by mixing the color wheel colors you've chosen with each other or with black and white paint.

❧ This dahlia uses the same analogous combination of yellow, yellow-orange and orange as the design above. It looks different because the color wheel colors have been toned with black and white. But notice that the combination is still very subtle. This project begins on page 54.

COMPLEMENTARY COLORS

Two colors that are directly across from each other on the color wheel are called complements. These are colors that are farthest away from each other on the color wheel and are therefore not similar. In fact, the combination of complementary colors creates the most contrast of any of the color combinations. Complementary colors enhance each other like no other color can—reds look redder and greens look greener when these complements are used together. Projects painted with complementary colors will be very dynamic and are wonderful if you really want to draw attention to the piece.

The complementary combination of red and green, above and at right, demonstrates the striking contrast you can incorporate into your painting.

🍂 *The tremendous amount of contrast between the dark green background and the red tulips really makes this piece stand out. This project, beginning on page 36, explains how complementary colors can also be used for shading.*

SPLIT COMPLEMENTARY COLORS

When you're ready to add a few more colors to your palette, try working with split complementary colors. This is a combination of a color and the color on each side of its complement. The color combinations may seem unusual. Who would have thought, for example, to use red-violet, yellow and green together, as shown in the design above? But the result is really quite pretty.

Using split complementary colors in your painting will produce an eye-catching piece with quite a bit of contrast.

This example of a split complementary scheme uses blue-green, orange and red. The result isn't quite as shocking as in the sample above because the colors are toned down considerably with black or earth tones (see page 23). Instructions for making this Hindeloopen plate are on page 124.

TRIADIC COLORS

My favorite combination of colors is the triadic. It consists of three colors spaced an equal distance (four spaces) apart on the color wheel. I like this combination because it opens up a much wider range of colors for my painting, especially when using the triadic of the primary colors. For me this triadic of yellow, blue and red is the most fun because, if I want to do a lot of mixing, I can use all the colors on the color wheel. In the example above I've stayed with mainly primary and secondary colors.

Other triadic combinations allow you to use a wide range of colors as well. The resulting painting will be high in contrast because, again, the main colors are spaced quite far apart on the color wheel.

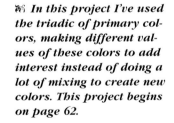

❧ *In this project I've used the triadic of primary colors, making different values of these colors to add interest instead of doing a lot of mixing to create new colors. This project begins on page 62.*

COLOR TERMS

The following are terms that you will help you to further your understanding of color.

Hue

Hue is simply the name of a color, such as red, blue or green. Although the colors below are different, they each are hues of red.

Alizarin Crimson   **Santa Red**   **Brilliant Red**

Temperature

Colors do have temperature—some are warm and others are cool. Generally speaking, warm colors are the colors found in the sun: reds, yellows and oranges. Cool colors are those found in the water: greens, blues and purples. The temperature of a color can really have an effect on its surroundings. For instance, try painting a room on the north side of your house with a warm color. Even with a lack of sunlight, the room will look warm and inviting. In contrast, painting a room on the south side of your house with cool colors will help counteract the harshness of direct sunlight.

Warm Colors

Cool Colors

❧ Warm colors are the colors of the sun. Cool colors are the colors found in the water.

TEMPERATURE IN YOUR DECORATIVE PAINTING

Using colors with different temperatures can help you create depth in your painting. Warm colors appear closer to the viewer, while cool colors appear farther away. Look at the plums at right. One plum in the center group is obviously on the bottom. Compared to the other plums in the group, this one is quite blue (a cool color) and that helps it to appear farther away from the viewer. I painted the next plum on the pile with slightly warmer colors, and warmed the colors even more for the top plum. Subtle variations in color like this really make some elements stand out and others recede.

As you're painting the projects in this book, look at which elements are warm and which are cool. The warmest elements will be those that come toward you and first catch your eye. The cooler elements will be those in the background and around the edges. These elements, such as fill flowers or leaves, add to the painting without detracting from the center of interest.

For the project at right, I used temperature to help show depth. The plums on top are painted in warm colors and look closer. The plums on the bottom are painted with cool colors and seem farther away. This project begins on page 106.

THE TEMPERATURE OF GRAY

Black + White = Cool Gray

Red + Green = Warm Gray

Black + White + Brown = Warm Gray

Even grays can have temperature. A gray created from black and white will be cool and can be used to shade cool colors. But a gray made from complementary colors or a gray made from black, white and burnt umber will be warm. Use these grays with other warm colors.

Tone and Value

Tone is the addition of black or white to an existing color to make it lighter or darker. Value is the lightness or darkness of a color. So, when you add tone to a color you change that color's value—the addition of white or black changes the lightness or darkness of the original color. Dark colors are said to have low values; light colors are said to have high values.

To see all the values of a color, it helps to make a value scale. At right are some value strips for black and Prussian Blue that I made by adding increasing amounts of white to the original color.

⚜ These strips show the different values of black (left) and Prussian Blue (right). They are shown from the lowest value to the highest.

⚜ Adding white to a color raises the value of the color. By adding white to the flower on the left, I made a lighter flower that has a higher value.

ᗕᗧᗕ TINTS ᗕᗧᗕ

⚜ Adding black to a color lowers the value of the color. Mixing black with the color on the right made this darker color with a lower value.

A tint is white with just a touch of color added. Because it is so close to white, a tint has a very high value. The temperature of a tint depends on the color that is added to the white. The pink tint above is warm because red, the color added to white to get pink, is warm. The blue tint is cool. Use tints to add a highlight to the tips of leaves and petals.

VALUE IN YOUR DECORATIVE PAINTING

To the eye, objects with light values appear bigger, while those with dark values appear smaller. Hold this page at arm's length and look at the two hearts at the right. Although the hearts are the same size, the light heart on the dark background looks a little larger. If you're painting a group of flowers and plan to have a light-value flower as the center of interest, keep in mind that, because of the value, the flower will naturally look larger than the others.

Value is also used to give dimension to painted objects. The yellow container below gets its rounded shape from the different values used to paint it. The darkest values are on the sides of the container—they almost blend into the background. As I moved toward the center of the container, I added lighter and lighter values, blending one value into the next. The highest value is in the front, where the container seems the roundest. To achieve this effect, you'll need about five values of a color, each blended carefully into the next. You can apply this technique to give dimension to any shape, whether it be an apple, a slice of watermelon or a flower vase.

The light heart above looks larger than the dark heart, but they are the same size. Objects with a lighter, or higher, value look larger than objects with a lower value.

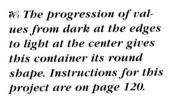

The progression of values from dark at the edges to light at the center gives this container its round shape. Instructions for this project are on page 120.

Intensity

Intensity describes the strength or saturation of a color. Is a color weak or strong, bright or dull, loud or soft? All twelve colors on the color wheel are strong, intense colors. The intensity of these colors can be reduced by adding toners such as black, white or earth tones (see page 23).

❧ *Adding white to red (or any color) lowers the intensity but also changes the value of the color.*

INTENSITY IN YOUR DECORATIVE PAINTING

The most intense color on the color wheel is red. Look at the vibrant red heart at the right for fifteen or twenty seconds. Then look away to a blank white piece of paper. You should see a green heart (red's complement) on the white paper. This shows what intense color does to the eyes—it's like your brain gets so full of red that it has to counteract it with its complement. You may have experienced this in your own painting, for example, if you've ever felt the need to take more frequent breaks when working on something that's very bright.

❧ *Staring at any intense color will saturate your brain, so when you look away, you will see that color's complement. After looking at this red heart for twenty seconds, you will see a green heart.*

The intensity of a color can be reduced by adding black or white. But adding one of these toners will change the value of the color as well. If you'd like to lessen the intensity of a color without changing the value, you can add that color's complement or an earth tone. This reduces the intensity without affecting the value because the two colors being mixed are of similar value. In the project at the bottom right, I wanted the small yellow flowers around the center of interest to be bright and intense, but I wanted the yellow flowers away from the center of interest to be more subdued. Both colors of flower have the same value, but the flowers around the edges are much less intense.

Be aware of intensity when painting with bright, strong colors. If it's a piece that you will look at a lot, you may want to lessen the intensity a bit so that it's restful to your eyes.

❧ *To lower the intensity of the yellow flowers farthest from the center of interest, I mixed the yellow with raw sienna. Instructions for this project are on page 122.*

Since prehistoric times, people have used minerals from the earth to paint. Copper, iron, manganese and others were used to create a variety of red, yellow and brown pigments. Some paints today still use minerals to create the colors yellow ochre, raw sienna, burnt sienna, burnt umber and raw umber. The strips below show the earth tones from the lightest value to the darkest. These colors are ideal for painting images of wood, like a barn door behind a chicken. They are dark and muted, so they're great for a background that won't detract from your center of interest.

Earth tones are also wonderful for lowering the intensity of a color without changing the value. Just add an earth tone with a value similar to the original color. To lower the intensity of a light pink, use a bit of yellow ochre; for a bright red, use burnt umber. If you're stumped as to which color to use, raw sienna will do the trick. You can tone down absolutely any color with a touch of raw sienna, as shown below.

◆● For lowering the intensity of a color, raw sienna is magic! No matter what color you start with, the addition of raw sienna can lower the intensity without changing the value.

❧ For each of the earth tones below, I have shaded the color using the next darkest earth tone (for raw umber, I shaded wth black). The detailing on each is the shading color plus black. You can use this simple formula for shading anytime you paint with earth tones.

Yellow Ochre

Raw Sienna

Burnt Sienna

Burnt Umber

Raw Umber

🥀 *The bright colors in the top row inspire playfulness and energy. The darker colors below are more somber and subdued.*

EMOTION

The various intensities of different colors evoke different emotions. Bright, clean colors like red, blue and orange create a happy, energetic feeling. Medium-intensity blues and greens can be peaceful and serene. Pastel colors feel soft and gentle.

Keep the emotion of the colors you are using in mind as you're painting or decorating your home. A living room with white walls, red carpeting and a black leather sofa will look stunning, but spending time with all these stimulating colors may make you tense and nervous. Even if you're only painting a picture for a room, keep in mind that room's purpose. A bedroom is an ideal spot for a picture with calming pastel flowers, not bright red ones. But be careful not to make things too somber and sad, either.

Contrast

Whether you're decorating a room, choosing an outfit or designing a painting, it is contrast, the differences between objects, that adds interest. A sofa covered with smooth fabric needs throw pillows with a textured weave. Dark pants or a skirt look much more striking with a light blouse. Warm against cool, light against dark, short against long, rough against smooth—all of these contrasts make whatever you're creating more interesting.

🥀 *The combination of red and green always provides contrast and interest, but other contrasts have been included in this design as well. Small touches, like placing some cherries higher than others or making some leaves bug bitten, add a lot of interest to this piece. This project begins on page 96.*

CONTRAST IN YOUR DECORATIVE PAINTING

Your use of contrast can make a big difference in your painting. Look at the rose on the warm yellow background. Now look at the rose on the cool blue background. The roses look as if they have been painted with different reds and pinks. Actually, they are exactly the same colors. The flowers look different only because of the background colors.

Shapes and sizes also provide contrast. When creating a bouquet of flowers, add buds and small fill flowers to contrast with the large flowers that are the center of interest. The edges of the cherry leaves on the box on the previous page provide some of the interest in that piece. Notice that some edges are brown, others are green; some edges have bug bites, others are smooth. Adding a few touches like these provides interest without being over-done.

🙠 The colors in the rose are the same in each picture. But the colors look different because of the contrast between the colors in the flower and the color of each of the backgrounds.

CENTER OF INTEREST

When an artist creates a design, she decides what will be the center of interest—the part of the design that will grab the viewer's attention and draw him into the painting. Temperature and intensity are used to pull the center of interest forward (warm colors and light values) and catch the viewer's eye.

The balance of a painting will also draw in a viewer, so placement of the center of interest is important. A painting with a center of interest in the middle or too far off to one side will not be as appealing as one with the center of interest passing through one of the "golden means." To find the golden mean, divide the surface into nine equal blocks—the places where four blocks meet are the golden means. A center of interest placed on one of these spots helps the painting to look balanced and attractive.

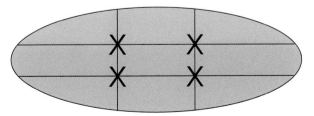

The center of interest should pass through one of the four intersections points created when you divide the surface into nine equal blocks.

CHAPTER TWO

Materials

1. Surface & Preparation Supplies

I like to use a variety of surfaces, such as wood, tin, glass, ceramic and plaster. The projects in this book can be transferred to any surface you desire. If your surface does not fit the pattern, you can just enlarge or reduce the pattern to fit. Remember, if the size of the pattern changes, you may need also to change the size of the brushes used to paint the project.

SURFACE PREPARATION
For wood, basecoat the surface with equal amounts of DecoArt Multi-Purpose Sealer and the acrylic paint color of your choice on a sponge brush. When dry, sand lightly using fine-grit sandpaper or a sanding oval. Wipe with a tack cloth to remove the sanding particles. Apply a second coat if necessary, but with paint only, not with a mix of paint and Multi-Purpose Sealer. When basecoating other surfaces, like metal or glass, sanding is not necessary.

When the base coat is dry, trace the project pattern onto tracing paper with a pencil. Position the traced pattern on the surface and secure with a piece of masking tape. Slip a piece of graphite paper between the pattern and the surface. Use a stylus to retrace the pattern onto the surface, then and remove the paper and tape.

2. Brushes

Good brushes are an artist's most important investment. I recommend you purchase a variety of high quality synthetic brushes, including rounds, flats, filberts and liners.

The brushes I use the most are Sandy's Easy Strokes, which I developed with Eagle Brush. I intended to use these for one-brush floral painting, but then I found that they worked great for basecoating and several different painting styles. Sandy's Mini Easy Stroke is similar to a no. 2 round, and Sandy's Easy Stroke is similar to a no. 4 round. The big differences between these brushes and other rounds are that the Easy Strokes have bristles that are a little shorter and barrels that are a little fuller. I use these brushes as flats as well. Just flatten out the brush on the palette before loading and use as you would any flat brush.

Once you've made the investment in brushes, be sure to take care of them. As you're painting, never leave the brushes in water. This can cause the paint to peel from the handle of your brush, and it allows too much water to be absorbed by the bristles. Rinse the brushes in cold water in a jar or a container with a smooth bottom. Use DecoMagic to clean fresh or dried paint from the bristles (although letting paint dry in the bristles is never a good idea). After you've cleaned the brushes, rinse with clean cool water and reshape the bristles to their original shape.

3. Paints

DecoArt Americana acrylic paint is my choice when it comes to painting. I like it because the colors are always the same—I know when I replace a bottle of color, the new bottle I open will be exactly the same as the old one. I also think the viscosity of the paints is wonderful. It's just right for strokes as well as basecoating. And the colors that are transparent are indicated on the DecoArt color chart, so we artists know which colors to use for glazing and shading.

You certainly could use your choice of brands of acrylic paint or even oil paint for any of the techniques in this book. Simply match the color swatches to your particular brand and type of paint.

4. Palette Paper

Like most decorative painters, I use a waxed paper palette for my paints. But I have found that when it comes to working with color, a gray palette, not white, can't be beat. I use the Athena Gray Palette. Like other palette paper, it is disposable, but it can also be wiped down after use to extend the life of the palette. The gray color provides a neutral background for your paints and allows you to see the colors more accurately than you would on a white background. You will not believe the difference until you actually see it with your own eyes.

5. Color Wheel

Now that you've learned how a color wheel works, you may find it handy to have one with your painting supplies. I use a color wheel from The Color Wheel Company. It's small enough to use when I'm painting or on the road, and it has templates to quickly illustrate which colors are complements, split complements, triadic and so on.

6. Finishing Supplies

After you've finished your project and all the paint has dried, remove any remaining pattern lines with a little odorless paint thinner on a paper towel, rubbing the towel on the surface to remove the lines. Another

method would be to use a white eraser to remove the lines.

To varnish a wooden surface, I apply two coats of DecoArt DuraClear Varnish using a large oval filbert brush. The filbert does not leave start and stop lines like a regular flat brush does. Allow the varnish to dry thirty minutes before applying a second coat. Two coats are sufficient. If I've used only regular acrylic paints on a project, I varnish it with DuraClear Satin Varnish. If I've used any metallic paints on a piece, I use DuraClear Gloss Varnish to really bring out the glow of the metallics.

On metal surfaces, I use DecoArt Americana Spray Sealer/Finisher in Gloss or Matte. If you use any spray finishers, follow the manufacturer's instructions and remember to spray outside, away from buildings, cars and plants.

PROJECT ONE
A Study in Monochromatic Colors

Winter Scene

BEFORE YOU CAN truly understand color, you need to understand values. This monochromatic project teaches you how to see and paint with values of color. Just think light, medium and dark—it's that easy. Remember the textures you make for the trees and snow are contrasts that make the painting even more interesting.

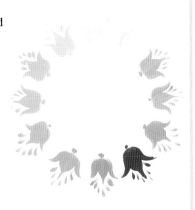

MATERIALS

Brushes
- 5/0 script liner
- no. 2 bristle fan
- ¼" (6mm) wing
- ¾" (19mm) flat

Additional Supplies
- vinegar
- DecoArt Brush 'n Blend Extender
- tracing paper
- pencil
- graphite paper
- stylus
- DecoArt Americana Matte or Gloss Spray Sealer/Finisher

Surface
- from Viking Woodcrafts

DecoArt Americana

Titanium (Snow)White   *Prussian Blue*   *Lamp (Ebony) Black*

Dark Background Mix: Prussian Blue + Lamp (Ebony) Black + Titanium (Snow) White (3:1:1)   *Medium Background Mix: dark background mix + more Titanium (Snow) White*   *Light Background Mix: medium background mix + more Titanium (Snow) White*   *Pond Mix: Prussian Blue + a touch of Lamp (Ebony) Black*

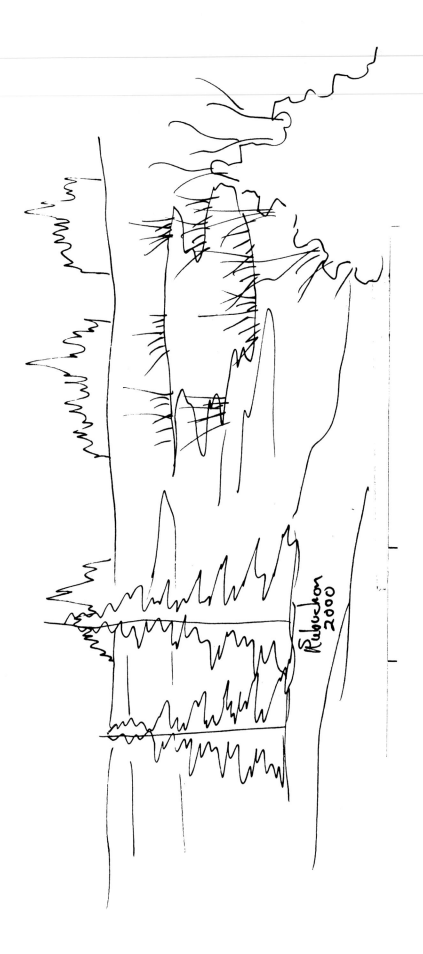

This pattern may be hand-traced or photocopied for personal use only. It appears here at full size.

❧ Background

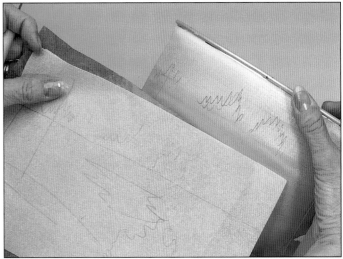

1 Wipe the metal container with a mixture of equal amounts of vinegar and water on a paper towel. Wipe dry with a clean paper towel. Load the ¾-inch (19mm) flat with the dark background mix and blending gel. Starting at the bottom, brush long strokes all the way around the piece using the full width of the brush. Add more Titanium White to the dirty brush (for the medium background mix) and continue working your way up the surface. Add even more Titanium White to the mix (for the light background mix) for the lightest value, to be placed toward the top of the piece.

2 Once the background has dried, transfer the pattern onto the surface with graphite paper and a stylus. The lines should be just dark enough to see clearly. After you do this project once you will probably find you do not need a pattern. Your imagination will do just fine.

❧ Background Trees

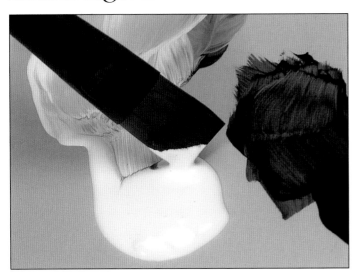

3 Load the flat brush with a mix similar to the dark background mix and some more blending gel. Dip one corner of the brush into the Titanium White; the white corner is for the tops of the trees.

4 Hold the brush handle vertical to the surface and dab on the trees in the background, keeping the white corner of the brush up.

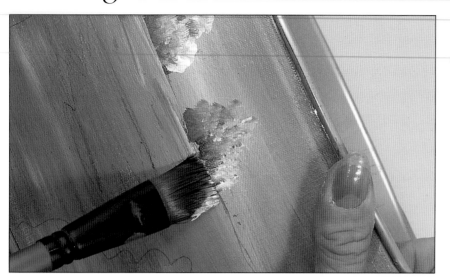

5 While the paint is still wet, add more blending gel to the dirty brush. Turn the bristles horizontal and make a long stroke along the bottom of each tree to blend them with the ground, then hit-and-miss a few strokes down the surface in front of the tree.

Do not clean the brush, just reload with the same colors, including the dab of white on one corner, and paint another group of trees as described beginning in step 4.

❧ *Pond*

6 Clean the flat brush and side load with a mixture of the pond mix and blending gel, pinching off the naked side of the brush to prevent the paint from working all the way across the brush. To do this, squeeze the bristles where they touch the metal ferrule and push up to the chisel edge. (The blending gel will allow the paint to slide easily on the surface.)

Hold the brush so the bristles are horizontal and the paint is on the outside edge of the pond. Make flowing, horizontal strokes to create the right side of the pond.

7 For the left side of the pond, turn the brush over so the paint is again on the outside and make flowing, horizontal strokes.

8 Using what little paint is left in the brush, zigzag some streaks of color across the center of the pond to the other side.

Ꮚ*Bush*

9 With the same technique and colors used for the background trees, dab in the bush in the foreground. Load the 5/0 script liner with Titanium White and paint in the weeds sticking out from the bush. These help to lead the eye back into the painting.

Ꮚ*Snow*

10 Clean the flat brush and place the bristles on the palette near a puddle of Titanium White. Push the tips into the edge of the paint so that you can scoop up the paint onto one side of the brush.

11 Turn the brush over to make sure there is no paint on the other side.

12 With the paint side up, dab the brush around one side of the pond to create snow. The large amount of paint on the brush gives the snow texture.

13 While the paint is still wet, dip a ¼-inch (6mm) wing brush in water, then pull up the Titanium White for grasses. Keep these grasses short, as they are in the background.

14 Use the same technique to create the snow on the other side of the pond. Add any final white details with the script liner.

❧Foreground Trees

15 Make a brush mix similar to the pond mix and thin with water. Load the script liner with this mix and paint the trunks for the trees in the foreground. This will help keep the trees straight as you add branches.

16 Load the no. 2 bristle fan brush with the same brush mix used for the trunks. Starting at the top of the tree, dab on the branches using just the corner of the brush.

17 As you work down the tree, use more of the fan brush to create the branches, so that at the bottom you're using the full width of the brush. Dab a second layer of branches on the tree with the same color paint and technique. This will make the tree look full and healthy.

18 Add Titanium White to the dirty brush and dab snow onto the right two-thirds of each tree to create dimension and interest.

19 Without adding more paint to the dirty bristle fan brush, set the trees into the scene by making horizontal strokes at the base and in patches in the foreground. Add hit-and-miss Titanium White highlights to the surface of the pond with the same brush. With the script liner loaded with a mix similar to the pond mix, pull up some dark grasses and branches around the pond and in the foreground snow.

20 To complete this project, remove any pattern lines, then varnish as described on page 26.

Tulips

FOR THIS PROJECT I present the subject—some pretty spring tulips—on two different-colored backgrounds to help demonstrate the power of complementary colors. When the red flowers are painted on the dark green background, the red looks much brighter. This is because red and green are complements and provide each other with the most contrast possible. On the off-white background the red tulips look much more subdued. Paint this project on whichever background color you like best.

MATERIALS

Brushes
- 5/0 script liner
- no. 4 round
- ¼" (6mm) wing
- no. 10 flat

Additional Supplies
- DecoArt Multi-Purpose Sealer
- sanding oval or fine-grit sandpaper
- tracing paper
- pencil
- graphite paper
- stylus
- DecoArt Faux Glaze Medium
- plastic shopping bag
- DecoArt DuraClear Satin Varnish

Surfaces
- from Walnut Hollow

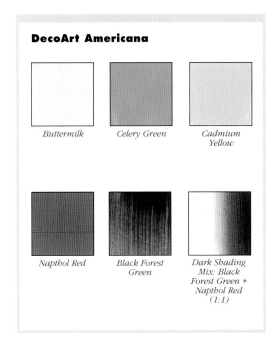

DecoArt Americana

Buttermilk	Celery Green	Cadmium Yellow
Napthol Red	Black Forest Green	Dark Shading Mix: Black Forest Green + Napthol Red (1:1)

Base Coat and Pattern

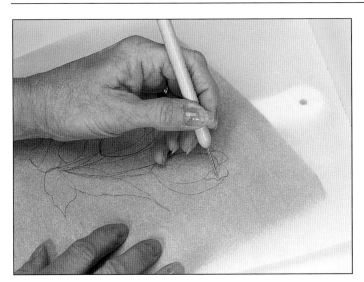

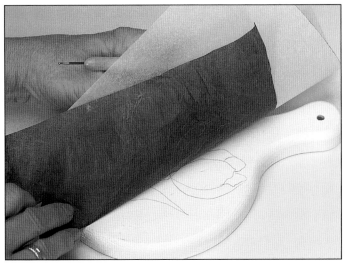

1 Basecoat the surface with either Black Forest Green plus an equal amount of Multi-Purpose Sealer or Buttermilk plus an equal amount of Multi-Purpose Sealer. When dry, sand lightly with a sanding oval. Copy the pattern onto tracing paper. Slip graphite paper underneath and retrace the pattern using a stylus to keep the lines thin and easy to cover.

2 After you begin tracing, lift the paper to be sure you have the right side of the graphite facing down on the surface. The lines should be just dark enough to see clearly.

Leaves

3 Basecoat each leaf with Celery Green using the no. 4 round brush. Leave the bottom left-hand leaf unpainted until after the stems have been placed. If painting on the green surface, follow these same instructions for painting the leaves. Because Celery Green is opaque, and will cover a dark color, there's no need to base in a lighter color first.

4 Dampen the no. 10 flat brush with water and blot lightly on a paper towel. Dip one corner of the brush into the puddle of Black Forest Green and blend on the pallette to achieve a nice float.

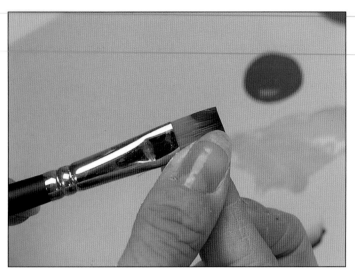

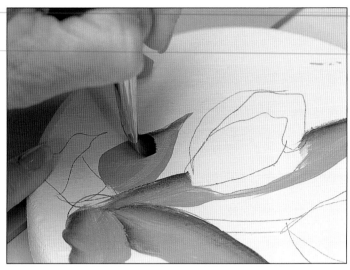

5 Before shading the leaves, pinch off the naked side of the brush to prevent the paint from moving across the width of the brush. To do this, squeeze the bristles where they touch the metal ferrule and pull up to the chisel edge.

6 Float the Black Forest Green down one edge of each leaf. Reload brush as needed.

7 With the chisel edge of the no. 10 flat, apply veins with Black Forest Green, first down the center and then on the sides.

8 Add a little Napthol Red to the dirty brush and paint warmer veins in between the green ones.

9 If you have used the green background, basecoat the flowers with Buttermilk and let dry. (The tulips do need to be basecoated with Buttermilk because the Napthol Red is translucent and would not cover the Black Forest Green.)

The tulips will be red. Since it's difficult to shade red without getting muddy, use red's complementary color, green, for the shading first, then basecoat with a transparent red. Side load the no. 10 flat with Black Forest Green, pinching off the naked side of the brush as shown in step five of this project. Add the first shading to the flowers where shown.

10 Let dry. Clean the flat brush and base each petal of the flower with Napthol Red, starting at the back and working your way to the front petal. Since Napthol Red is transparent, it allows the shading and the pattern to show through, even if multiple coats of Napthol Red are applied.

11 When the base coat is dry, side load the flat brush with the dark shading mix and add the deepest shading to the tulips.

12 Thin Cadmium Yellow with water and load a little on the ¼-inch (6mm) wing brush. Starting with the front petal, hold the brush straight up and pull down very lightly from the edge of the petal. Use only a little paint and a very light touch. Without reloading the brush, do the same to the side petals of that same flower.

13 Reinforce the yellow highlights by repeating the previous step, using the same paint color and brush.

14 Let dry, then thin a bit of Buttermilk with water and, with the wing brush, apply the lightest highlights to only the front petal of each tulip.

15 Load the 5/0 script liner with Napthol Red and outline the tulips hit-and-miss to crisp up the edges and cover any pattern lines. Be careful not to make continuous lines along the edges of the petals; this will make your flowers look unnatural. Add little lines into the petals from the edge, too.

❧Stems

16 Now that the flowers are complete, add the stems. Flatten the round brush and load with Black Forest Green. Add a little Cadmium Yellow to one flat side of the brush. Start at the base of the flower and pull the flattened brush down. Following steps 3 through 8, add the bottom, left-hand leaf in front of the stems.

❧Finishing Touches

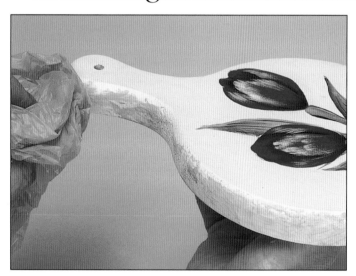

17 Side load the flat brush with thinned Celery Green. With the loaded side toward the leaves, float the color along the bottom edge of the plant to set the design onto the surface.

    For the border of the Buttermilk piece, mix equal amounts of Celery Green and glazing medium. Dampen the sides and top edge of the surface with water. Crumple the shopping bag and dab it into the mix. Tap the bag on the palette to soften and then tap it onto the dampened surface. Dampening a surface before applying a faux finish allows you to wipe off the paint if you've made a mistake.

18 When the piece has completely dried, remove pattern lines with a white eraser or with paint thinner on a paper towel.

19 For the border on the piece with the Black Forest Green background, I simply painted the edge with Celery Green using a no. 4 round. Because the piece itself has such a decorative shape, I didn't feel it needed anything more.

To complete either of these projects, varnish as described on page 26.

PROJECT THREE
A Study in Triadic Colors

Strokework Bird

NOT ONLY DOES THIS cheerful bird give you an opportunity to work on your strokes, it demonstrates the use of triadic colors. Varying shades of red, yellow and blue are used to create this easy and colorful piece. The bottled colors listed below lessen the need to brush mix colors as you go. Have fun with your painting, and eventually the right colors will come to you.

MATERIALS

Brushes
- 5/0 script liner
- no. 2 round
- no. 4 round
- ¾" (19mm) flat

Additional Supplies
- vinegar
- DecoArt Multi-Purpose Sealer
- tracing paper
- pencil
- dark graphite paper
- stylus
- DecoArt DuraClear Satin Varnish

Surface
- from Viking Woodcrafts

DecoArt Americana

Light Buttermilk	*Antique White*	*True Ochre*	*Raw Sienna*	*Cadmium Red*	*Santa Red*
Burgundy Wine	*Jade Green*	*Arbor Green*	*Dark Pine*	*Country Blue*	*Admiral Blue*
Camel	*Medium Flower Mix: True Ochre + Camel (1:1)*	*Light Flower Mix: medium flower mix + Light Buttermilk*	*Bird Detail Mix: Admiral Blue + a touch of Dark Pine*		

Base Coat and Border

Wipe the metal container with a mixture of equal amounts vinegar and water on a paper towel. Wipe dry with a clean paper towel. With the ¾-inch (19mm) flat (or any brush you feel comfortable with), base the container with equal amounts of Antique White and Multi-Purpose Sealer. Apply a second coat of Antique White only if necessary. Use a no. 4 round brush to paint the trim areas with Dark Pine.

When dry, transfer the pattern with dark graphite paper using a stylus to keep the lines thin and easy to cover.

With the flat, float Country Blue around the inside of the oval, keeping the color to the outside edge.

Load the 5/0 script liner with Dark Pine (see Tip), and paint scrolls around the edge of the oval. Wipe the brush and add a few strokes of Arbor Green.

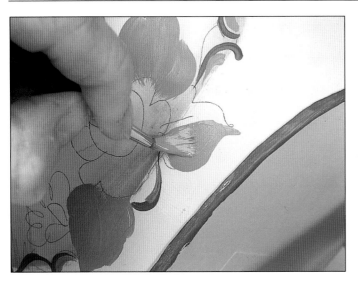

2 Basecoat the leaves with Arbor Green using the no. 4 round brush.

3 Again load the script liner with Dark Pine, and outline one side of each leaf with hit-and-miss lines. Touch-and-pull veins toward the center on the other side of each leaf.

TIP

For easy comma strokes, thin the paint with water to an ink-like consistency and fill the brush up to the metal ferrule. Then dip just the tip into unthinned paint. Touch the tip to the surface and pull. The heavy unthinned paint will come off the brush to form the head of the comma and the thinned paint will automatically make a thin tail.

4 With the Dark Pine on the script liner, add small touch-and-pull filler leaves around the large leaves. Clean the script liner and load with Jade Green. Paint S-stroke veins on each leaf opposite the Dark Pine veins. Then go over the filler leaves with Jade Green, partially covering the Dark Pine, to make these leaves less harsh.

5 Load the no. 4 round with Burgundy Wine. Starting in the back row of a fill flower, touch the brush down on the top of a petal and lift as you pull down toward the center of the flower. Paint only the back row of petals with Burgundy Wine.

6 Wipe the brush and load with Santa Red, the middle value for the flowers. Using the same technique as in step five, paint in the next row of petals, making shorter and fewer strokes in-between and over the Burgundy Wine strokes.

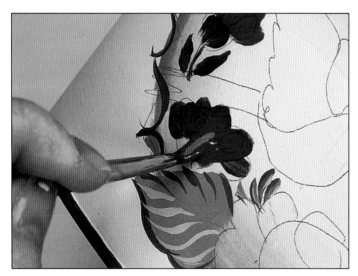

7 Wipe the brush again and load with Cadmium Red for the lightest value. Paint the front row of petals, making these even fewer in number and shorter.

8 Add Dark Pine to the dirty brush and form the calyx with one comma stroke on the right and another on the left. Pull a curved line for the stem and add a few leaves.

🍂Large Flower

For the large yellow flower, load the no. 4 round (or the no. 2 round if you prefer) with True Ochre, a middle value. Again pull the strokes from the outside, lifting the brush toward the center. Pull strokes from the bottom toward the center as well. Create a nice, full flower with these strokes.

Wipe the brush and add Camel for the medium flower mix. As with the red flowers, make fewer and shorter strokes. Wipe the brush again, add Light Buttermilk for the light flower mix and paint a few highlights. Basecoat the top center with Raw Sienna. When dry, add dots of Light Buttermilk with the handle end of the brush. Place tiny dot flowers of True Ochre in the same way.

🍂Bird

Basecoat the bird's body with a mix similar to the medium flower mix on the no. 4 round. Dip one corner of the brush in a little Light Buttermilk and apply to the bottom of the belly.

Flatten out the dirty brush and side load with a little Santa Red. Float the color down the bird's back.

12 Basecoat the back wing and the tail with Country Blue on the no. 4 round. Add a little Admiral Blue to the brush and shade down the right side of the wing and on the underside of the tail.

13 Load one side of the dirty brush with just a little Light Buttermilk. Stand the brush straight up at the tip of the wing, then touch-and-pull soft highlight feathers. Paint a few of these highlights on the tail as well.

14 Basecoat the front wing with Country Blue, add Admiral Blue to the brush and shade the wing as shown. Add Light Buttermilk to the brush and use the touch-and-pull technique to make the highlight feathers. To help this wing come forward in the painting, add more feathers than you did to the back wing.

15 Load the script liner with the bird detail mix to add the final details to the bird. Paint the bill, the top of the head, the eye and the line around the eye. With the handle end of your brush, add a dot of Light Buttermilk for the glint in the eye and dots of Light Buttermilk on the bird's belly.

❧ Finish

16 To complete the project, remove any pattern lines, then varnish as described on page 26.

PROJECT FOUR
A Study in Analogous Colors

Dahlia

To PAINT THIS dahlia, I used the analogous colors of yellow, yellow-orange and orange, mixed to varying degrees with black and white. If you prefer, you can choose colors that are already mixed in the bottles or tubes. However, I'd like you to see how easy it is to brush mix these colors as you go along. On the next page, I demonstrate how to build all the colors used in this project from just a few bottled paints.

MATERIALS

Brushes
- 5/0 script liner
- no. 2 round
- ¾" (19mm) flat
- 1" (25mm) foam brush

Additional Supplies
- vinegar
- DecoArt Multi-Purpose Sealer
- tracing paper
- pencil
- white or light graphite paper
- stylus
- DecoArt Faux Glaze Medium
- plastic shopping bag or sponge
- DecoArt Americana Matte Spray Sealer/Finisher

Surface
- from Brushworks

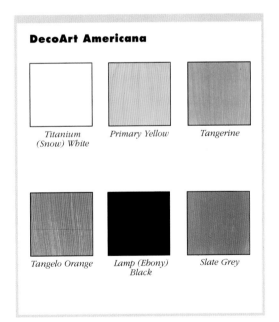

DecoArt Americana

Titanium (Snow) White	Primary Yellow	Tangerine
Tangelo Orange	Lamp (Ebony) Black	Slate Grey

Leaves

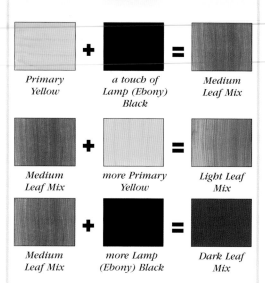

| Primary Yellow | + | a touch of Lamp (Ebony) Black | = | Medium Leaf Mix |

| Medium Leaf Mix | + | more Primary Yellow | = | Light Leaf Mix |

| Medium Leaf Mix | + | more Lamp (Ebony) Black | = | Dark Leaf Mix |

Flowers

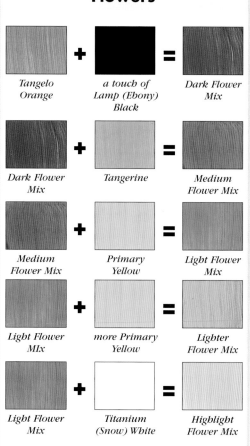

| Tangelo Orange | + | a touch of Lamp (Ebony) Black | = | Dark Flower Mix |

| Dark Flower Mix | + | Tangerine | = | Medium Flower Mix |

| Medium Flower Mix | + | Primary Yellow | = | Light Flower Mix |

| Light Flower MIx | + | more Primary Yellow | = | Lighter Flower Mix |

| Light Flower Mix | + | Titanium (Snow) White | = | Highlight Flower Mix |

Faux Finish

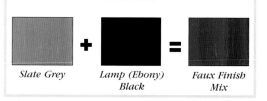

| Slate Grey | + | Lamp (Ebony) Black | = | Faux Finish Mix |

Mixing Colors

I know mixing colors can be intimidating, but I'd like you to give it a try to see how easy it is. Just place your puddles in a row, according to value, and mix the colors as you paint the project. It's not an exact science, so don't worry if your mix doesn't match these swatches exactly—that just helps to make the project uniquely your own!

When brush mixing color, as for the flowers in this project, place your puddles of paint in a vertical row from darkest to lightest. As you progress to the lighter shades of petals, add in lighter colors of paint. This picture shows how your palette will look as you prepare to add the lightest petals.

Brush mixing makes only a small amount of mixed color. Mixing a whole puddle of color will lose the interest of varying colors each time you mix.

Base Coat and Leaves

1 Wipe the metal tray with a mixture of equal amounts vinegar and water on a paper towel. Wipe dry with a clean paper towel. Basecoat the surface with Slate Grey using a foam brush. When dry, transfer the pattern onto the surface with a stylus and white or light graphite paper.

Load the no. 2 round with the medium leaf mix. Paint the leaves with comma strokes, keeping a little space between the leaves so that you can come back and add more of a different color.

Add more Primary Yellow to the dirty brush (for the light leaf mix) and stroke on lighter leaves mainly around the center of interest, in this case the large flower. Clean the brush and, with the dark leaf mix, place a few dark strokes for the leaves that are farthest away from the center of interest. Use the same colors for the stems.

Dahlia Petals

2 Load the 5/0 script liner with the dark flower mix. Press lightly on the brush to form the end of the petal, then lift the brush as you pull toward the center. Make some petals long and others short; keeping the petals varied in size and direction makes the flower look more natural.

3 Add Tangerine to the dirty brush for the medium flower mix and paint petals in-between the dark ones. Again, vary the lengths, making some petals quite short and others long enough to reach the edge of the flower.

4 Add Primary Yellow to the dirty brush for the light flower mix and paint more petals of different lengths, but do not extend any petals to the edge. For the lighter flower mix, add more Primary Yellow to the brush. Add a lot of petals with these two colors to make your flower full and healthy.

5 Finally, add a little Titanium White to the mix for the highlight flower mix. As you paint these lightest petals, let them be shorter and a little more delicate than any of the previous petals.

Bud Petals

6 The flower buds are similarly done but are not quite as light as the flower because the sunlight has not yet begun to fade out the colors. Begin making petals with the dark flower mix. Add Tangerine for a medium flower mix and stroke in a few petals, and finally add Primary Yellow (for the light flower mix) for the lightest petals.

❧Dahlia Center

7 Basecoat the center of the flower with a mix similar to the dark flower mix. Add a dot of Primary Yellow for the very center. With Lamp Black on the script liner, make small comma strokes in a ring around the center. Paint the strokes behind the center longer than those in front of the center.

❧Bud Calyxes

❧Stems

8 To finish the buds, load the no. 2 round with a mix similar to the medium leaf mix. Make three small comma strokes to form the calyx, positioning the surface so that you can pull the strokes toward yourself. With the same mix, complete the calyx with a small oval at the base.

9 Pull stems from the flower and each bud, add filler leaves and make any other adjustments with this green mix. Load the liner brush with white and make a small dot on each of the black strokes around the center of the flower.

10 Complete the border by mixing the faux finish mix with three parts glazing medium. Apply this mix to the rim of the plate with the ¾-inch (19mm) flat brush. Dab the wet paint with a crumpled plastic bag or a dampened sea sponge.

To complete this project, remove any pattern lines, then varnish as described on page 26.

PROJECT FIVE
A Study in Triadic Colors

Russian Roses

GLAZES ARE USED in this project to create depth and interest in the petals and leaves. The triadic color scheme with primary colors really shines on the black background. The gold accents add the final touch of old-world elegance.

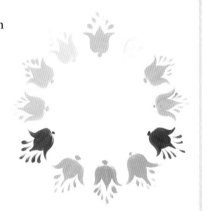

MATERIALS

Brushes
• 5/0 script liner
• no. 4 round
• no. 6 filbert
• ¾" (19mm) flat
• large soft mop brush
• 2" (51mm) foam brush

Additional Supplies
• DecoArt Multi-Purpose Sealer
• DecoArt Faux Glaze Medium
• tracing paper
• pencil
• white graphite paper
• stylus
• DecoArt DuraClear Gloss Varnish

Surface
• Brushworks

DecoArt Americana

| Titanium (Snow) White | Cadmium Yellow | Raw Sienna | Napthol Red | Alizarin Crimson | Avocado | Evergreen |

Prussian Blue *Lamp (Ebony) Black* *Olde Gold* *Leaf Base Mix: Avocado + a touch of Prussian Blue* *Leaf Shading Mix: Evergreen + a touch of Prussian Blue* *Leaf Highlight Mix: Cadmium Yellow + a touch of Prussian Blue* *Dark Fill Flower Mix: Prussian Blue + a touch of Titanium (Snow) White*

DecoArt Dazzling Metallics

Medium Fill Flower Mix: dark fill flower mix + more Titanium (Snow) White *Light Fill Flower Mix: medium fill flower mix + more Titanium (Snow) White* *Yellow Flower Mix: Cadmium Yellow + a touch of Alizarin Crimson* *Blue Flower Mix: Prussian Blue + a touch of Evergreen* *Medium Blue Flower Mix: blue flower mix + Titanium (Snow) White* *Medium Red Flower Mix: Napthol Red + a touch of Titanium (Snow) White*

Glorious Gold

These patterns may be hand-traced or photo-copied for personal use only. They appear here at full size. The top pattern is used for the border on top of the lid. The bottom pattern is used for the sides of the lid.

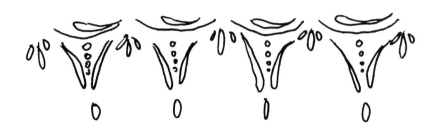

❧ Background

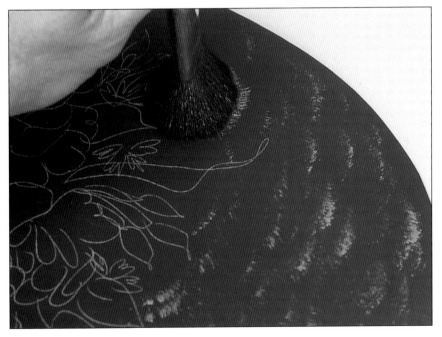

1 Basecoat the entire surface with equal amounts Multi-Purpose Sealer and Lamp Black using the foam brush. Let dry. Transfer the pattern onto the surface with a stylus and white graphite paper.

Spread the bristles of the large mop brush near the puddle of Glorious Gold. Carefully push just the tips of the bristles on one side of the brush into the paint.

2 Pounce small amounts of paint on the surface, keeping the brush perpendicular to the surface and splaying the bristles. Dab the paint heavier toward the outside edges and lighter as you move into the pattern area.

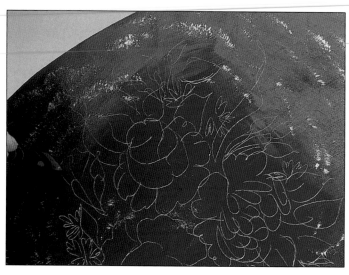

3 When dry, make a brush mix of one part Alizarin Crimson and two parts glaze medium. With the ¾-inch (19mm) flat, brush the glaze over the areas painted with gold.

4 Basecoat the leaves with the leaf base mix on the no. 6 filbert brush. Let dry. Dampen a section of leaves with a little water and shade the leaves with a filbert loaded with the leaf shading mix. Shade one side of each leaf and, to soften, lightly brush over the line where the basecoat color and shading color touch. Shade each of the leaves, working in sections to keep the surface damp.

5 Clean the filbert brush and, when the shading is dry, again dampen a section of leaves with a little water. With the leaf highlight mix, highlight the leaves using the filbert, pulling strokes from the vein area to the edge of the leaf.

6 Load the 5/0 script liner with Raw Sienna and detail the leaves with hit-and-miss linework. Add this linework to one side of each leaf or the other and down the centers of some leaves for the vein and stem.

❧ Fill Flowers

7 Load the no. 4 brush with the dark fill flower mix. Make one touch-and-pull stroke down the center of each petal, then pull one shorter stroke on each side of the center. The three strokes together make up one petal, and several petals make a flower.

8 Add a little more Titanium White to the dirty brush for the medium fill flower mix. Place a second layer of shorter strokes on only the petals closest to the center of the design.

❧ Flower Buds

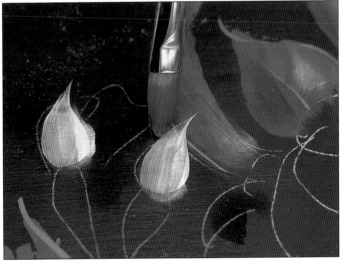

9 Add more Titanium White to the dirty brush (for the light fill flower mix) and highlight just a stroke or two on each flower, placing highlights over the medium blue petals only. Basecoat the center of each blue flower with Raw Sienna and, with the tip of the script liner, add dots of Olde Gold.

10 Basecoat the pink buds with Titanium White on the filbert brush. Clean the brush and shade the buds with Alizarin Crimson thinned with a bit of water.

❧ Flower Buds (continued)

11 To ensure these elements stay in the background, complete all the leaves, filler flowers and buds before starting the large flowers.

❧ Large Flowers

12 Base the three large flowers with Titanium White using the round brush, taking care to follow the contours of each flower. Allow to dry.

❧ Yellow Rose

13 Dampen the top right-hand flower with water using the ⅜-inch (19mm) flat brush. With the yellow flower mix, shade the flower with the filbert brush, following the contours of the flower. Leave the bottom two-thirds of each petal along the skirt of the flower unpainted.

14 When dry, add the second shading using the same brush and paint mix. Paint the entire flower this time. While this is still wet, add Titanium White and just a little Cadmium Yellow to the dirty brush. Place this color on the skirt of the flower and in the center portion. Follow the contours of the flower as before, but lift the stroke before you cover up all the base color.

❧ Blue Mum

15 Dampen the mum on the top left with a little water. Shade with the blue flower mix on the filbert brush, again leaving the bottom two-thirds of the skirt petals white. Allow to dry. Dampen again and apply a second shading, this time painting the entire flower. Add Titanium White to the dirty brush (for the medium blue flower mix) and stroke on the middle value, taking care not to cover up all of the shading.

❧ Red Rose and Highlights

16 The red rose is painted as described for the yellow and blue flowers, using Alizarin Crimson for the base color and Napthol Red and a little Titanium White for the medium red flower mix. After all the flowers have dried, dampen with water and apply Titanium White for the final highlight. Highlight only the front half (or the half closest to the center of the design) for each flower. Cover up half the flower with your hand if it helps you to visualize where to place the highlight.

❧ Flower Linework

17 For linework around the flowers, add just a bit of the flower color to the Titanium White and thin to an inklike consistency; the color for the linework should be lighter than the main color of the flower. Crisp up the edges of the flower with hit-and-miss outlining.

Finish the centers of the red and yellow roses with a few dots each of Raw Sienna and Cadmium Yellow.

❧Leaf and Flower Glaze

18 Mix one part Prussian Blue with two parts glazing medium. With the flat brush, paint the glaze over three or four leaves near the edge of the design. Mix a yellow glaze (see Tip), and add a little "sunshine" to a few leaves or petals near the center of interest.

TIP

Adding glaze to an element such as a petal or leaf can make that element either come forward or recede back into the design, depending on the color of the glaze. A blue glaze will make an object darker and cooler and push it to the background. A red or yellow glaze will make an object warmer and brighter and move it into the foreground. Glaze can be used all over a petal or leaf or just down one side. I like to mix one part color to two parts glazing medium, using Alizarin Crimson for red glaze, Cadmium Yellow for yellow glaze, and Prussian Blue for blue glaze. Remember, if you mix red and yellow glaze together you will get orange. If you mix red and blue glaze together you will get purple.

❧Border Linework and Side of Box

19 With white graphite paper and a stylus, trace the pattern for the design on the lid and sides of the box, repeating the pattern to go all the way around the box. Thin Glorious Gold with a little water to achieve an ink-like consistency. Load the script liner and make comma strokes to cover the pattern lines.

If you wish, you may freehand the linework on the lid. Just mark the the distance in from the edge and the distance between strokes with a soapstone.

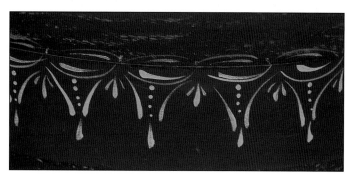

20 For the side of the lid, make the strokes face in the opposite direction. Add descending dots and additional comma strokes for a decorative border.

21 The design on the bottom of the box is the same as was described in steps 1 through 3.

22 To complete this project, remove any pattern lines, then varnish as described on page 26. A gloss varnish will really make the gold glow.

PROJECT SIX
A Study in Analogous Colors

Grapes

COLOR CAN HELP tie your background faux finish to the subject of your painting. In this piece, the Black Plum in the background is used again for the darkest grapes. This project also demonstrates the analogous color scheme of violet, blue-violet and red-violet.

As you're painting these grapes, pay particular attention to the reflected light. Remember that reflected light always falls away from the light source.

MATERIALS

Brushes
- 5/0 script liner
- no. 4 round
- ¼" (6mm) wing
- ¾" (19mm) flat
- no. 10 flat

Additional Supplies
- DecoArt Faux Glaze Medium
- small sea sponge
- tracing paper
- pencil
- dark graphite paper
- stylus
- DecoArt Brush 'n Blend Extender
- DecoArt DuraClear Satin Varnish

Surface
- from Catalina Cottage

DecoArt Americana

Titanium (Snow) White | Sand | Camel | Arbor Green

Admiral Blue | Black Plum | Dark Grape Mix: Black Plum + a touch of Admiral Blue + a dot of Titanium (Snow) White | Medium Grape Mix: dark grape mix + more Titanium (Snow) White

Light Grape Mix: medium grape mix + more Titanium (Snow) White | Dark Shading Mix: Black Plum + a touch of Admiral Blue | Right Highlighting Mix: Titanium (Snow) White + a touch of Black Plum | Left Highlighting Mix: Titanium (Snow) White + a touch of Admiral Blue

2 Mix one part Black Plum with eight parts glazing medium.

1 Basecoat the surface with Sand. When dry, use the ¾-inch (19mm) flat to cover the surface with glazing medium. Let this dry.

3 Dampen the sea sponge with water and dab it into a little of the Black Plum mixture. Tap the sponge on the palette until the pattern that the sponge produces looks lacy.

4 Dab the sponge lightly all over the surface, creating random light, medium and dark values. Add more of the paint mixture to the sponge as necessary, remembering to tap it on the palette before applying it to the surface.

5 Add a little more color around the top of the container. When dry, transfer the pattern with dark graphite paper and a stylus.

❧Grapes and Leaves

6 Basecoat the leaves with Camel on the no. 10 flat brush. Basecoat the bottommost grapes with the dark grape mix on the no. 4 round.

7 As you work your way up the pile, the color of the grapes becomes lighter. Add more Titanium White to the dark grape mix to get the medium grape mix and basecoat the mid-level grapes. Add considerably more Titanium White to get the light grape mix for the lightest grapes at the top of the pile.

With the no. 10 flat brush, use a little blending gel and shade Arbor Green around the outside edges of the leaves.

8 Float a little Black Plum on the leaves, hit-and-miss, as a burnish (a darkness along the edge of a leaf).

Load the dark shading mix on the no. 10 flat. Place this shading where grapes overlap each other, starting at the bottom of the pile and moving up.

9 Side load the no. 10 flat with the right highlighting mix. Float this color with a little blending gel down just the outside edge of each grape on the right half of the cluster. For the grapes on the left side of the cluster, side load the brush with the left highlighting mix and shade the left side of these grapes.

Begin to detail the leaves with thinned Black Plum on the script liner.

10 Continue to detail the leaves, adding veins and hit-and-miss outlining with thinned Black Plum.

11 Load the script liner with either highlighting mix and outline some of the grapes with hit-and-miss lines to shape up any flat or bulging grapes. Load a little Titanium White onto the ¼-inch (6mm) wing brush and lightly paint a soft highlight onto some of the grapes. Use the corner of the wing to add a highlight dot to other grapes.

12 Add a few tendrils with thinned Black Plum on the script liner. Basecoat the stem with the no. 4 round loaded with thinned Black Plum. Add a spot of Titanium White at the very top of the stem.

To complete this project, remove any pattern lines, then varnish as described on page 26.

PROJECT SEVEN
A Study in Triadic Colors

Carnations

THIS PROJECT IS a great example of how deep, vibrant colors can gradually change to soft and light with the addition of white. For these carnations, you will start with bright primary colors on one side of the brush and white on the other. As you complete the strokes to make one flower, the white will work its way into the color and make it pastel.

The design is an asymmetrical one, with a C shape on the left side and an S on the right. Use the ferns to help the design flow and direct the eye where you want it to look.

MATERIALS

Brushes
- no. 2 round
- no. 4 round
- ¾" (19mm) flat

Additional Supplies
- DecoArt Multi-Purpose Sealer
- plastic shopping bag
- DecoArt Faux Glaze Medium
- tracing paper
- pencil
- graphite paper
- stylus
- DecoArt DuraClear Gloss Varnish

Surface
- from Designs by Bentwood

DecoArt Americana

Titanium (Snow) White

Desert Sand

Celery Green

Lt. Avocado

Olde Gold

Napthol Red

Prussian Blue

Dark Leaf Mix: Celery Green + a touch of Prussian Blue

Leaf Detail Mix: Celery Green + Prussian Blue + a touch of Titanium (Snow) White

Red Flower Mix: Napthol Red + a touch of Lt. Avocado

Bud Mix: Napthol Red + Prussian Blue (1:1)

Fern Mix: Lt. Avocado + Prussian Blue (1:1)

DecoArt Dazzling Metallics

Glorious Gold

This pattern may be hand-traced or photocopied for personal use only. Enlarge at 111 percent to bring it up to full size.

❧ Background

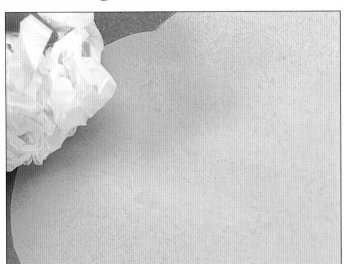

❧ Leaves

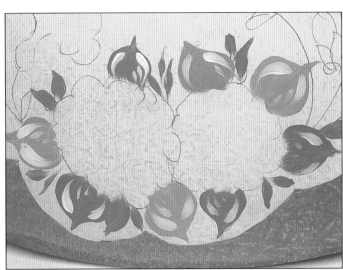

1 Basecoat the surface with a brush mix of equal parts Desert Sand and Multi-Purpose Sealer on the ¾-inch (19mm) flat. When dry, transfer the border pattern onto the surface with graphite paper and a stylus. Paint the outer area and sides of the lid with Lt. Avocado on the flat brush. Let dry.

For the faux finish, dampen the surface with a little water on the clean flat brush. Brush mix one part Celery Green with three parts glazing medium and apply over the damp area using the flat brush. Immediately dab the surface with a crumpled plastic shopping bag so that the bag lifts some of the paint mix, leaving a mottled pattern. Allow to dry before transferring the full pattern to the surface with graphite paper and a stylus.

2 Load the no. 4 round brush with Celery Green. Basecoat a few of the leaves, starting at the tip end of the leaf. Add just a little Prussian Blue to the brush to make the dark leaf mix, and paint a few darker leaves. Add more Celery Green or Prussian Blue, whichever you prefer, to complete the leaves. Varying the color like this adds just a little interest to the leaves, making some of them warm and others cool. Use the same colors to make small strokes for filler leaves.

Load the no. 4 round with the leaf detail mix and paint comma strokes on the large leaves—make quite a few strokes before reloading the brush to get a variation in color. Vary the size of the strokes as well.

❧ Red Flower

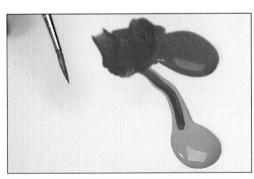

3 Fill the no. 2 round brush all the way to the ferrule with the red flower mix. (The mixture of green and red, complementary colors, reduces the intensity of the red, toning it down a bit for the flowers.)

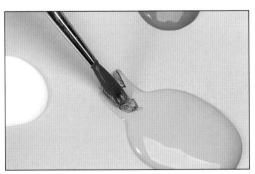

4 Flatten out the round brush and pull three sweeps of Olde Gold out onto one side.

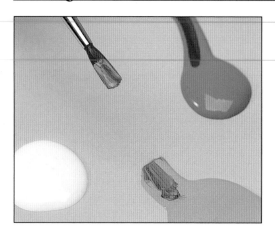

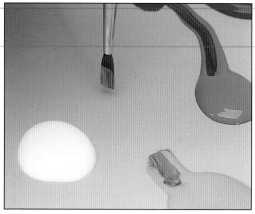

5 Lift the brush up and away from the puddle and turn it over to see that the Olde Gold is on one side of the brush.

6 Place the brush on the far side of the puddle of Titanium White, with the gold side facing the puddle.

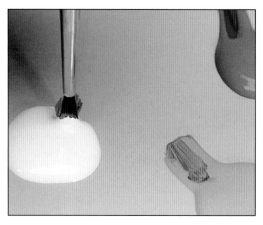

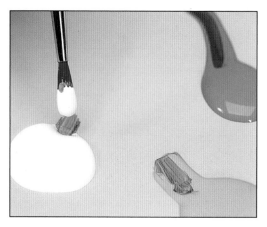

7 Place the brush near the puddle of paint. Press the brush against the puddle to get a "glob" of Titanium White on the brush, on top of the Olde Gold.

8 Lift the brush out of the paint. Note that the white paint is on top of the gold.

9 Keeping the white side of the brush up and the red side on the surface, set the tips of the brush down slightly inside the pattern line for the flower.

10 Wiggle the bristles of the brush open to no more than one-quarter of a circle. Lift the ferrule of the brush so that it does not touch the surface.

11 Push the brush forward slightly until the bristles extend just beyond the paint that was on the surface as a result of fanning out the bristles.

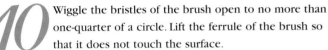

Gold Flower

12 Pull the brush back to where you started and lift the brush from the surface. Lift another glob of Titanium White and make the next petal, placing the petals as described in steps 13 through 16.

13 For the gold flower, load the brush with Olde Gold, then flatten the brush and pull three strokes of the red flower mix onto one side of the brush. Pick up a glob of Titanium White on the red side of the brush, as described previously.

To begin a flower, place the first petals at the outside edge at north, south, east and west, loading more white on the brush after each petal.

14 Fill in with more petals to complete the outer circle of petals.

15 Work toward the center of the flower, filling in row two with more strokes, adding more Titanium White after each petal.

16 For the third and final row, make only three or four petals. Add a little Olde Gold to the dirty brush and dab in a few stamen dots in the very center.

Clean the brush before starting each flower, but once the brush is filled with color, add only Titanium White before making each petal.

❧ Blue Flower in Profile

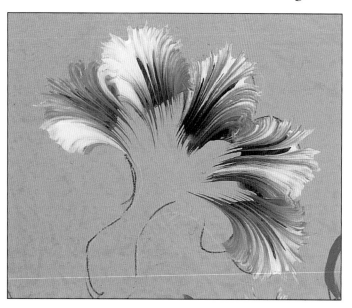

17 Clean the brush, load with Prussian Blue and lift in Titanium White, using the same technique as described above. Fill in the back row of the small flower with five petals. As before, start the strokes inside the pattern line so that the flower doesn't get too large.

18 Fill in the second row with three petals, starting with the center petal.

19 Complete the petals by adding one petal to the third row. Add Lt. Avocado to the dirty brush for the calyx. Turn the flower upside down and, starting at the stem end, pull the brush toward yourself to form one-half of the calyx. Repeat for the other half. Pull the stem down from the calyx using the same dirty brush. Add a few filler leaves to the stem.

Flower Buds

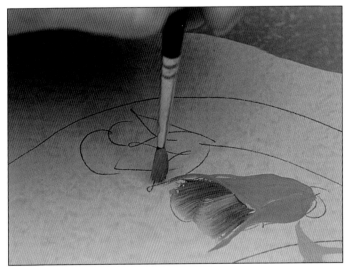

20 The buds can be done with colors of your choice; here I use Prussian Blue for one and Napthol Red and Prussian Blue for the other. For the first bud, load the no. 4 round brush with Prussian Blue, then pull three strokes into the Titanium White. Keep the white side up and fan the brush open just slightly. Pull the brush straight down toward the stem. For the second stroke of the bud, place the brush so that it overlaps the original petal.

21 Add Lt. Avocado to the dirty brush and stroke on the calyx, starting at the stem end and pulling the stroke toward yourself. Add stem and filler leaves. By adding green to the dirty brush you are able to tie the bud to the calyx with color.

Flower Buds (continued)

22 For the second bud, load the brush with the bud mix of Napthol Red and Prussian Blue plus three strokes of Titanium White. Make two strokes for the bud, as described in step 20. Add Lt. Avocado to the dirty brush and paint the stem and a few filler leaves.

Ferns

23 For the fern by the blue flower, fill the no. 4 round with Lt. Avocado. Make the brush flat and pull three strokes of Prussian Blue on one flat side. Turn the brush over and pull three strokes of Titanium White onto this side (opposite the blue). Paint a long comma stroke for the top leaf and continue the tail down to make the stem of the fern. Make two smaller strokes in this direction, then continue down that side of the stem, making comma strokes in the opposite direction. The strokes down the other side of the stem all face the same direction as the top comma stroke. Do not reload the brush while painting this fern; let the diminishing amount of paint add variety to the leaves.

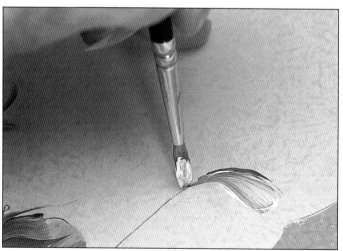

24 For the fern by the buds, fill the no. 4 round with the fern mix. Flatten the brush and add more Prussian Blue to one side of the brush, then add Titanium White on top of the Prussian Blue. Start the fern with a large comma stroke.

25 Continue the tail of the comma stroke down to form the S shape of the stem. As in step 23, paint two smaller comma strokes to the left of the first stroke, then switch directions and continue down the left side of the stem. For the right side, paint small strokes in the same direction as the top stroke.

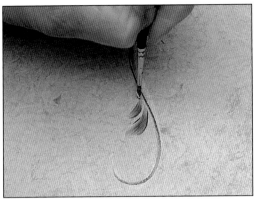

26 The strokework around the side of the box is similarly done. Load the no. 2 round with Lt. Avocado, then flatten the brush and add Prussian Blue to one side. Add a little Titanium White to the other side of the brush. Paint a thin S-shaped line for a stem. Add a large comma stroke at the center of the S-shaped line and another, smaller stroke below that.

27 Continue painting the comma strokes, making them smaller as you work toward the ends of the line, but do not paint strokes all the way to the end. Reverse the direction of the comma stroke for the other side of the stem.

28 Repeat this fern design around the box. The cool green leaves of the fern border offer contrast to the warm background. Contrast makes color more interesting.

29 Clean the no. 2 round and load with Glorious Gold. Use this to paint a border on the top of the lid where the Desert Sand and Lt. Avocado touch.

To complete this project, remove any pattern lines, then varnish as described on page 26.

PROJECT EIGHT
A Study in Tetradic Colors

Wild Roses

ON THE COLOR wheel, a tetrad is made up of four colors: one color from each side of two complementary colors. In this project I've used the colors on either side of yellow-green and red-violet—the tetrad of yellow, green, red and violet.

This soft S-shaped design is pleasing to look at; the curves at either end bring your eye back into the center of the design. The small dark fill flowers help create a back plane and offer an interesting contrast to the large, lighter flowers that are the center of interest.

MATERIALS

Brushes
• 5/0 script liner
• no. 4 round
• no. 12 flat
• ¾" (19mm) flat
• 1" (25mm) foam brush

Additional Supplies
• DecoArt Multi-Purpose Sealer
• sanding oval or fine-grit sandpaper
• tracing paper
• pencil
• white graphite paper
• stylus
• DecoArt Faux Glaze Medium
• sea sponge
• DecoArt DuraClear Satin Varnish

Surface
• from Designs by Bentwood

DecoArt Americana

Titanium (Snow) White	Golden Straw	Cherry Red	Avocado	Royal Purple	Lamp (Ebony) Black

Leaf Base Mix: Avocado + a touch of Lamp (Ebony) Black	Leaf Detail Mix: Golden Straw + Cherry Red + Avocado (2:1:1)	Dark Flower Mix: Royal Purple + a touch of Titanium (Snow) White	Medium Flower Mix: dark flower mix + a touch of Cherry Red	Light Flower Mix: Cherry Red + a touch of Titanium (Snow) White + a touch of Avocado	Medium Shading Mix: Avocado + a touch of Lamp (Ebony) Black

Dark Shading Mix: medium shading mix + more Lamp (Ebony) Black	Light Linework Mix: Titanium (Snow) White + a touch of Cherry Red	Medium Linework Mix: Titanium (Snow) White + a touch of Royal Purple	Flower Center Mix: Cherry Red + Avocado (1:1)	Fill Flower Mix: Cherry Red + Royal Purple (1:1)

𝄐Base Coat and Leaves

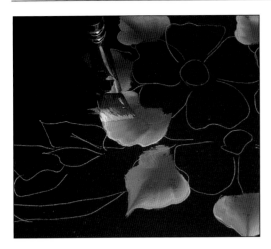

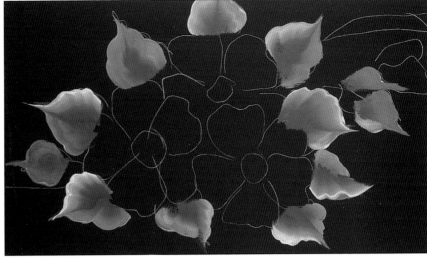

1 Basecoat the entire surface with equal parts Lamp Black and Multi-Purpose Sealer using a foam brush. When dry, sand lightly. Basecoat surface again with just Lamp Black. When dry, transfer the pattern with white graphite paper and a stylus.

For the leaves, load the no. 12 flat with the leaf base mix. Dip one corner of the brush in a very small bit of Golden Straw and blend the float on the palette. Keeping the light corner of the brush to the edge of the leaf, start at the stem end of the leaf and wiggle the light edge down one side of the leaf. Use the darker corner of the brush as a pivot. Repeat the process for the other side of the leaf. Paint a few leaves before you reload the brush.

2 Add a little Titanium White to the light side of the dirty brush and blend the colors on the palette. Keeping the white to the outside, highlight the very edge of some of the leaves for variation. Then dip the dark side of the brush in Avocado, blend on the palette and float the color down the very edge of a few other leaves.

TIP

*B*y using a limited palette and mixing colors that you need, you know the colors you mix will be compatible with the rest of the painting. However, if you prefer, you may use bottled paints. For example, the brush mix in step 3 could be replaced with Raw Sienna.

𝄐Flower Petals

3 Load a wet script liner with the leaf detail mix. Pull center veins on the leaves, positioning the piece so that you can pull the veins from the base of the leaf toward yourself. Hit-and-miss a line along one edge of each leaf.

4 Basecoat the flowers and buds with Titanium White using the no. 12 flat brush. Let dry.

5 Start with the darkest flower. Side load the no. 12 flat with the dark flower mix. Blend the brush on the palette so that the color is on only one edge of the brush. Paint the petals, leaving a bit of white around the outside edge. Some days you paint light and other days you paint dark. Work the color until it pleases you.

6 Add a bit of Cherry Red to the dark flower mix (to get the medium flower mix) and side load this mix on the no. 12 flat. Blend on the palette, keeping the paint on one corner of the brush. Paint the midvalue flower with the color toward the edge of the petal. Paint the buds with this same color, leaving very little of the white base coat showing (see step 16 on page 94).

Side load the no. 12 flat with the light flower mix (a dustier pink due to the addition of green) for the third flower. As before, keep the color toward the outside.

7 Add shading to each flower, beginning with the lightest. Side load Avocado on the ¾-inch flat brush and shade the flower, keeping the colored side of the brush toward the center. Add a bit of Lamp Black to the Avocado (the medium shading mix) for the shading on the medium flower. Again, keep the paint on one edge of the brush and the color toward the center of the flower. Add even more Lamp Black (the dark shading mix) to the mix and shade the darkest flower.

8 Clean the ¾-inch flat brush. Side load the brush with Titanium White and apply hit-and-miss strokes along the edges of the petals. Use more Titanium White on the lightest flower and less Titanium White as you work back to the darker flowers.

9 Load the script liner with the light linework mix. Add linework along the edges of some petals of the lightest flower, going from narrow to wide and back to narrow so it looks like the edge of the petal is flipped. Do the same for the other flowers, using the medium linework mix. Add less linework to the darkest flower.

❧ Flower Center

10 With the no. 4 round brush, dab the flower center mix on the center of each flower. The brush mix should resemble raw sienna, but because it is a combination of the colors on the palette, it will look more natural in this painting than color straight from a bottle.

11 Add just a little Golden Straw to the dirty brush and paint a ring of dots in the center of each flower.

12 When dry, side load the no. 12 flat with a little Lamp Black and float around the centers.

❧ Tendrils and Leaves

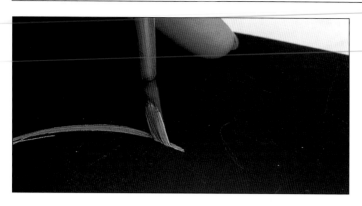

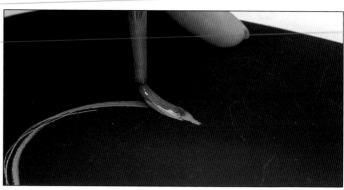

13 Load the no. 4 round with a brush mix similar to the dark shading mix. Flatten the brush and pull just a little Golden Straw onto one side of the brush. Using the chisel edge of the brush, pull a long, thin line for the stems. For the leaves, stand the brush perpendicular to the surface and lightly touch the tip of the brush to the surface.

14 Press the brush down to create a slight bulge as you pull the brush toward the stem.

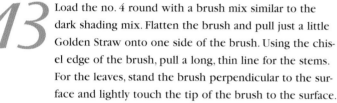

15 Lift the brush as you continue pulling toward the stem. Add more leaves down each of the stems using this same technique.

❧ Fill Flowers and Bud Calyxes

16 Load the round brush with the fill flower mix. Press and pull a few small petals for each flower, painting only a few full flowers. Load the script liner with a brush mix similar to the flower center mix and make small dots for the stamens.

Load the round brush with a brush mix similar to the dark shading mix for the calyx of the buds. Flatten the brush and add just a little Golden Straw to only one side of the brush. Keeping the Golden Straw side up, begin the stroke by the petals and pull down to the stem. Turn the brush so the gold side is down for the second stroke. Clean the brush and reload for the second calyx.

Finally, load the script liner with Titanium White thinned with water, and paint dots around the center of each large flower. Clean the brush and repeat with thinned Lamp Black.

17 For the sides of the lid, first dampen with water using the ¾-inch flat brush. Dab the sea sponge into Avocado, then into Lamp Black and then into glazing medium. Tap the sponge several times on the damp surface before reloading it with more paint.

18 To complete the project, remove any pattern lines, then varnish as described on page 26.

PROJECT NINE
A Study in Complementary Colors

Cherries

IN THIS PROJECT, which uses the complementary colors of red and green, I have tried to make the most of the available space and to make the piece visually appealing at the same time. Overlapping two cherries not only saves space, it is much more interesting to look at. Keep in mind, too, that a design must have space around the edge for the viewer to rest his or her eye. The larger the design, the more you need a place to rest your eyes.

An important element of this design is the use of shadow. There are two kinds of shadows: cast shadows and body shadows. Cast shadows fall away from the light source and assume the shape on which they fall. (In this project, the cast shadows are flat because they fall on a table.) They reflect color and light, and must have three values of cool color. Body shadows fall toward the light source and assume the shape that is casting the shadow. They are narrow, warm in temperature and one value darker than the object on which they fall.

Reflected light appears only on round or cylindrical objects and is opposite the light source. It is cool in temperature and medium in value.

MATERIALS

Brushes
- 5/0 script liner
- no. 2 round
- no. 8 flat
- ¾" (19mm) flat
- mop brush
- 2" (51mm) foam brush

Additional Supplies
- DecoArt Multi-Purpose Sealer
- DecoArt Brush 'n Blend Extender
- tracing paper
- pencil
- white graphite paper
- stylus
- DecoArt Faux Glaze Medium
- DecoArt DuraClear Satin Varnish

Surface
- from Walnut Hollow

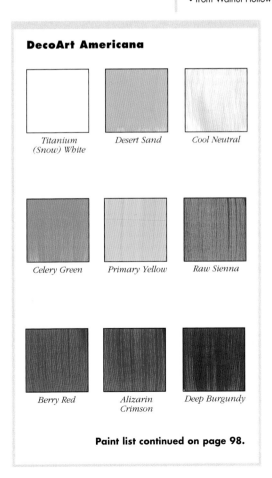

DecoArt Americana

Titanium (Snow) White	Desert Sand	Cool Neutral
Celery Green	Primary Yellow	Raw Sienna
Berry Red	Alizarin Crimson	Deep Burgundy

Paint list continued on page 98.

DecoArt Americana, continued

Avocado

Evergreen

Prussian Blue

Asphaltum

Leaf Highlight Mix: Primary Yellow + Celery Green (1:1)

Burnish Mix: Evergreen + Raw Sienna + Deep Burgundy (1:1:1)

Cherry Base Mix: Berry Red + Titanium (Snow) White (1:1)

Highlight Mix: Berry Red + Primary Yellow (1:1)

Reflected Light Mix: Titanium (Snow) White + a touch of Prussian blue

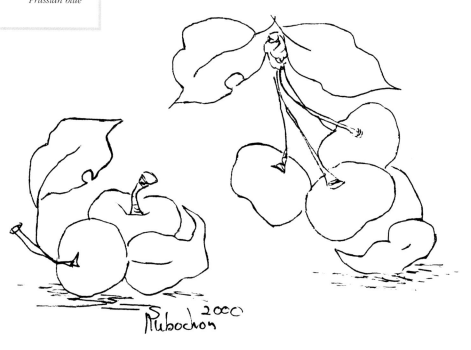

*❧ **This pattern may be hand-traced or photocopied for personal use only. It appears here at full size.***

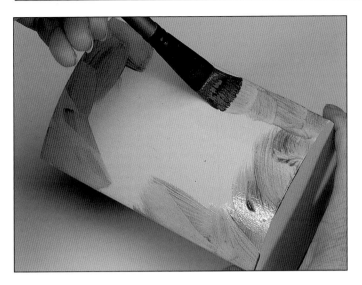

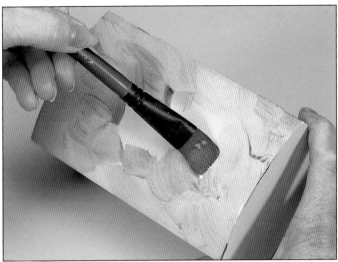

1 Basecoat the surface with equal parts Desert Sand and Multi-Purpose Sealer on the foam brush. When dry, make a brush mix of equal amounts of blending gel and Asphaltum. With the ¾-inch (19mm) flat, brush this mix onto the corners and edges of the piece, picking up more paint and medium as needed.

2 Add Raw Sienna to the dirty brush. Again, start at the edges and work the color in toward the center.

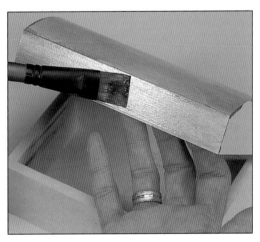

3 Add Desert Sand to the dirty brush. Working from the center out, add Desert Sand until you're satisfied with the color in the center of the piece. If you'd like the edges to be a little darker, add more Asphaltum to the brush and reapply.

4 Paint the sides of the lid with the brush mix of Asphaltum and blending gel on the ¾-inch (19mm) flat, using long, sweeping strokes. Check the top periodically to make sure the mix doesn't accumulate. When dry, transfer the pattern onto the lid with white graphite paper and a stylus.

Leaves

5 Basecoat the leaves with Avocado on the no. 8 flat. Side load the brush with Evergreen and shade down each leaf on the side nearest the outside edge of the piece. For the highlights, side load the dirty brush with Celery Green. Float the color on the three background leaves on the side of each leaf that is nearest the center of the design. For the two front leaves, add the leaf highlight mix to the dirty brush, blend and float highlights on each. When painting the highlights, keep the loaded side of the brush toward the center of the leaf.

Bug Bites and Burnishes

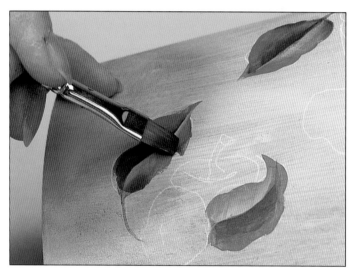

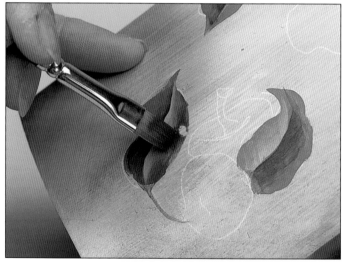

6 To add bug bites and burnishes to some of the leaves, side load the no. 8 flat with the burnish mix. For a bug bite, slide the brush forward and back to form a C.

7 Flip the brush over and again slide the brush forward and back to form a C. The color is transparent, so repeat this step and the previous one as necessary to punch up the color.

8 For a burnish, just float the same burnish mix down the edge of the leaf. The bug bites and burnishes add interest to the leaves, but overdoing the flaws will eliminate the contrast and interest.

9 Basecoat the cherries with the cherry base mix on the no. 8 flat. When dry, basecoat again with Cherry Red using the same brush.

10 Dip one corner of the dirty brush in Deep Burgundy. Walk the float out on the palette, then float Deep Burgundy down both sides of each cherry.

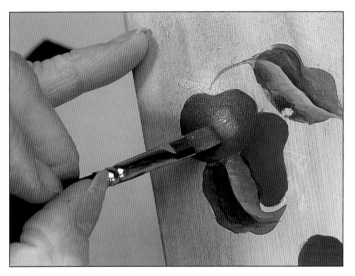

11 Where two cherries touch, apply a second float of Deep Burgundy to the touching edge of the background cherry. This is the body shadow, and it helps to separate one cherry from another.

12 When dry, dampen the cherries with a bit of water. With the cherry highlight mix on the no. 8 flat, place the highlight color on the medium-value area of each cherry. The highlight should not touch the darkest value.

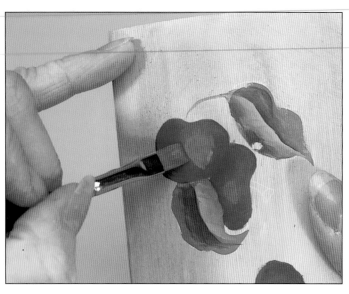

13 Wipe the brush and pat off the edges of the highlight, blending the edges into the medium value. Apply the highlight a second time if you wish; I reinforced the highlight for the middle cherry in the grouping of three because it is the center of interest.

14 Clean the no. 8 flat and side load a mix similar to the burnish mix. Float the color in a small partial circle where the stem attaches to the cherry.

15 Use this same brush and paint to place a float on the edges of the background cherries.

16 Clean the no. 8 brush and side load with the reflected light mix. Apply a small float to the left-hand side of each cherry for the reflected light.

17 With the no. 2 round, paint the stems with Asphaltum, then add Raw Sienna to the dirty brush and apply a medium value to the stem. Finally, add Titanium White to the dirty brush and add highlights to the stem.

Cast Shadow

18 Side load the ¾-inch (19mm) flat with Asphaltum. Float a cast shadow under each object that is to be resting, keeping the paint side of the brush toward the object.

Cherry Highlights

19 Add a Titanium White highlight to the rounded part of the most exposed cherries with a 5/0 script liner.

🎔 Final Adjustments

20 Make any final adjustments to your painting. If you feel the colors on the cherries aren't blended enough, apply a red glaze to help unify them. Make a brush mix of one part Alizarin Crimson and two parts glazing medium. Brush this onto the cherries with the no. 8 flat. Reapply the Titanium White highlights if they are no longer bright enough.

🎔 Faux Finish on Sides of Box

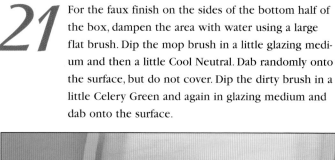

21 For the faux finish on the sides of the bottom half of the box, dampen the area with water using a large flat brush. Dip the mop brush in a little glazing medium and then a little Cool Neutral. Dab randomly onto the surface, but do not cover. Dip the dirty brush in a little Celery Green and again in glazing medium and dab onto the surface.

22 Add a little Evergreen, Raw Sienna and glazing medium to the brush at one time and dab onto the surface. Without adding more paint to the brush, pat the center of each side to blend and soften the color. Pat around the edges less so that the outside is left darker and more distinct.

23 Finish with a little more Evergreen and glazing medium on the dirty brush.

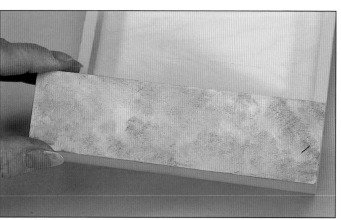

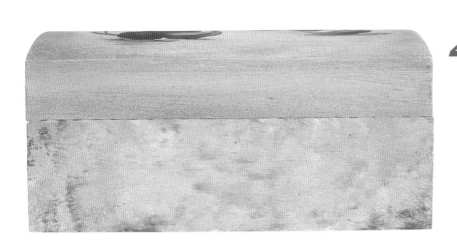

24 Continue to work the color, patting to soften, until you're satisfied with the result.

25 To complete this project, remove any pattern lines, then varnish as described on page 26.

PROJECT TEN
A Study in Split Complementary Colors

Plums

T HE SOFT C CURVE in this design leads the eye around the tray. The colors I've selected are a split complementary of yellow, red-violet and blue-violet. The warmest plum is on top and as the plums get deeper into the design and farther away from the center of interest, they become darker. To keep the blossoms in the back plane, paint them with dull, dirty colors. Adding a colored glaze to some of the leaves pushes them into the back plane as well.

MATERIALS

Brushes
- 5/0 script liner
- no. 4 round
- no. 8 filbert
- no. 10 flat
- ¾" (19mm) flat

Additional Supplies
- vinegar
- tracing paper
- pencil
- white or light graphite paper
- stylus
- DecoArt Faux Glaze Medium
- DecoArt Brush 'n Blend Extender
- small sea sponge
- DecoArt Americana Matte Spray Sealer/Finisher

Surface
- from Brushworks

DecoArt Americana

Titanium (Snow) White	Yellow Light	Red Violet	Blue Violet	Neutral Grey	Lamp (Ebony) Black

Medium Leaf Mix: Yellow Light + Blue Violet + a touch of Lamp (Ebony) Black

Dark Leaf Mix: Blue Violet + a touch of Lamp (Ebony) Black + a touch of Yellow Light

Light Leaf Mix: Yellow Light + a touch of Blue Violet

Raw Sienna Mix: Yellow Light + a touch of Red Violet + a touch of Blue Violet

Flower Base Mix: Titanium (Snow) White + a touch of Yellow Light + a touch of Blue Violet

Flower Shade Mix: medium leaf mix + a touch of Titanium (Snow) White

Flower Wash Mix: Yellow Light + Red Violet (1:1)

Dark Plum Mix: Red Violet + Blue Violet + a touch of Lamp (Ebony) Black

Medium Plum Mix: dark plum mix + more Red Violet

Light Plum Mix: medium plum mix + more Red Violet

Reflected Light Mix: Titanium (Snow) White + a touch of Blue Violet

Plum Glaze Mix: Red Violet + Blue Violet (1:1)

❧ Base Coat and Leaves

1 Basecoat the entire surface with Lamp Black. When dry, transfer the pattern with white or light graphite paper using a stylus to keep the lines thin and easy to cover.

Basecoat the leaves with the no. 4 round brush filled with the medium leaf mix. Fill in the leaf shapes with as few strokes as possible; this will keep the leaves smooth.

When dry, dampen with water (see Tip). Load the no. 8 filbert with the dark leaf mix and apply it down one side of center to place the color, then make two soft strokes to blend where the two colors meet. If you can see the entire leaf, apply the shading down the side of the leaf that is closest to the edge of the design. If the leaf goes under another leaf or petal, apply the shading color across the stem.

2 When dry, dampen as before and load the filbert with the light leaf mix. Pull soft comma strokes down the side opposite the shading. Paint a few leaves before reloading the brush so you get a variation in the color. Finish the leaves with hit-and-miss linework using the thinned raw sienna mix on the 5/0 script liner.

TIP

*D*ampen metal surfaces with water, but dampen wood surfaces with blending gel (wood will just absorb the water).

❧ Branches

3 Load a mix similar to the raw sienna mix on the round brush and use it to paint the branches. Add Titanium White to the dirty brush for highlights. Dip the dirty brush in Lamp Black if you'd like to add some dark shading.

TIP

*B*rush mixing the shading and highlight colors, instead of using bottled colors, varies the colors and makes them interesting.

4 Basecoat the blossoms with the flower base mix, pulling the brush from the tip of the petal toward the center of the flower. To shade the blossoms, side-load the no. 10 flat with the flower shade mix. Float the color around the center of the flower, keeping the naked side of the brush toward the outside. These are just fill flowers, so keep them dark.

5 When dry, load the round brush with Titanium White. Dampen the blossoms with water and place a small, soft high-light petal on top of some of the petals closest to the center of interest. With the no. 10 flat, mix the flower wash mix with glazing medium and brush over some of the petals, particularly those away from the center of interest. Vary the petals by brushing the glaze over some of those you had highlighted.

6 With the script liner, dab the centers of the blossoms with the raw sienna mix used for the leaves and branches. Clean the brush and add a few dots of Yellow Light to the center. Add one tiny dot of Red Violet for the very center.

7 Basecoat the plums with Titanium White using the round brush flattened out. Allow to dry. Dampen the plums with water. With the filbert brush, apply the dark plum mix to the plum farthest from the center of interest, following the contours of the fruit. Apply with pressure to keep the color where you put it, and lightly blend while it's still wet. Leave some areas on curves unpainted. Add more Red Violet to the brush mix (to get the medium plum mix) and paint the plum in the middle ground using the same techniques. Add more Red Violet to the mix (for the light plum mix) for the plum on the top, which is the center of interest.

8 When the first shading is dry, dampen the area and apply the shading a second time, using the same colors. Again, leave the areas on the curve unpainted.

9 While the surface is still damp, add Titanium White to the dirty brush, blend on the palette to a middle value and fill in the unpainted areas.

10 When dry, dampen the area again. With the filbert brush, add a highlight of Titanium White to each plum using a small amount of paint. Apply this highlight at least once more to reinforce the color.

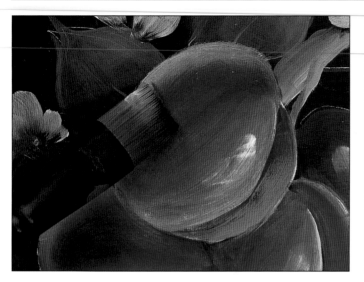

11 Side load the ¾-inch (19mm) flat with the reflected light mix. Float this mix down the left side of each plum to create the look of reflected light.

12 Make a glaze for the plums with one part plum glaze mix and two parts glazing medium. Use the ¾-inch (19mm) flat to apply the glaze lightly to all of the plums. It's more effective to apply a little bit of glaze several times than to apply a lot of glaze once. I usually apply two layers of glaze. Let the glaze dry in-between layers.

You can also vary the glaze slightly, adding more red to the plums at the top of the pile (because warm colors come forward) and more blue to the plums at the bottom.

❧ *Leaf Glaze*

❧ *Border*

14 A dull, light border on this dark background will keep the viewer's eye in the painting without detracting from it. Mix one part Neutral Grey with two parts glazing medium. Dip the sponge into the mix and pat it on the palette before applying to the edge of the plate. Tap the sponge lightly onto the surface until you're happy with the result.

13 Glaze the leaves with one part either Blue Violet or Red Violet and two parts glazing medium. Apply the blue glaze to leaves you want to recede into the background, and the red glaze to those you'd like to come forward. Glaze only some of the leaves, for variety.

15 Apply stems to the plums using a mix similar to the raw sienna mix. With the filbert brush, add a final highlight of Titanium White to the two center plums. To complete this project, remove any pattern lines, then varnish as described on page 26.

TIP

The addition of varnish to a painted piece can really change its look, especially on dark surfaces like this one. If you'd like to get a better idea of what a piece will look like when varnished, brush it with clean water.

Gallery of More Ideas

Border Flowers

A Study in Triadic Colors

ON A TRAY or any surface on which objects will be placed, a border can be the center of interest for your painting. In this design, the flowers are warm in the center of each side and become smaller and cooler toward the corners. The faux finish in the middle rounds out the piece.

Preparation

Clean the metal as described in step 1 on page 31. Base the surface with a brush mix of Antique Teal and Multi-Purpose Sealer. Transfer the pattern with white graphite and a stylus.

Faux Finish

Dampen the center area with water. Brush mix one part Viridian Green with two parts glazing medium and dab on surface. Add one part Black Green with two parts glazing medium to the dirty brush and fill in remaining areas. Tear a 2-inch piece of cardboard and wiggle it around in a curve. Lift and repeat. Outline curves with a pencil eraser.

Flowers and Leaves

Base the center flowers with Orchid, then float Alizarin Crimson around the center area. Highlight with Light Buttermilk. Base the center with Raw Sienna; highlight with just a touch of Titanium White. Finish with Alizarin Crimson, Black Green and Light Buttermilk in the center. Base the tulips with Violet Haze and shade with Dioxazine Purple. Highlight with a brush mix of Light Buttermilk and just a touch of Violet Haze floated down the outside edges of each petal. Float Dioxazine Purple across the bottom of each tulip. Make dots using the handle end of your brush in Royal Purple for the corner flowers. Once dry, make a smaller dot of Violet Haze on top of the Royal Purple dots.

Fill the round brush with Black Green and add three pulls of Avocado. Keep the Avocado side up and pull leaves toward the stem. Add linework of thinned Raw Sienna to edge of each leaf.

Finish as described on page 26.

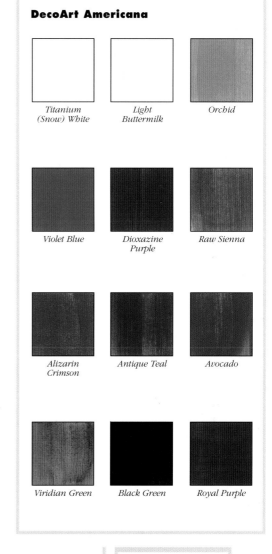

DecoArt Americana

Titanium (Snow) White	*Light Buttermilk*	*Orchid*
Violet Blue	*Dioxazine Purple*	*Raw Sienna*
Alizarin Crimson	*Antique Teal*	*Avocado*
Viridian Green	*Black Green*	*Royal Purple*

MATERIALS

Brushes
- 5/0 script
- no. 2 round
- no. 6 flat
- no. 10 flat
- ¾" (19mm) flat

Additional Supplies
- vinegar
- DecoArt Multi-Purpose Sealer
- DecoArt Faux Glaze Medium
- cardboard
- tracing paper
- pencil
- white graphite paper
- stylus
- DecoArt Americana Matte Spray Sealer/Finisher

Surface
- from Catalina Cottage

❀ *This pattern may be hand-traced or photo-copied for personal use only. Enlarge at 132 percent to bring it up to full size.*

RATHER THAN JUST fill in the bottom part of this clock with flowers, I used a soft L-curved design for added interest. The dark, curved lines allow your eye to move down the piece to the brighter colors in the center of interest. For this project I've used the complementary colors of red-orange and blue-green.

PREPARATION

Base with a brush mix of equal parts Antique Teal and Multi-Purpose Sealer. When dry, sand lightly. Apply a second coat of just Antique Teal. Base the border around the edge with Lamp Black. When dry, transfer the pattern with white or light graphite paper.

LEAVES

Fill the flat brush with Arbor Green. Edge one corner of the brush into Buttermilk and blend on the palette. Stroke on the leaves, keeping the light corner of the brush to the edge of the leaf. Use less Buttermilk on leaves that are farther away from the center of interest.

FLOWERS

For the dark flowers away from the center of interest, fill the round brush with Heritage Brick and stroke on the darker petals. Add Gingerbread to the dirty brush and paint shorter and lighter strokes over the dark petals.

For the lighter flowers in the center of interest, fill the round brush with Gingerbread and paint the petals. Add Buttermilk to the dirty brush and stroke shorter, lighter petals over the Gingerbread.

Add the stems and calyxes using the same technique and colors as for the leaves.

Dab the centers of the flowers with Marigold. Add a touch of Lamp Black to the centers as they get farther away from the center of interest. Add stamen dots with the 5/0 script liner, first with Lamp Black, then with Antique Teal.

With the round brush, paint the small fill leaves with a brush mix of Antique Teal and Lamp Black. Use this same mix for the tendrils.

Finish as described on page 26.

DecoArt Americana

Buttermilk · Marigold · Gingerbread

Heritage Brick · Arbor Green · Antique Teal

Lamp (Ebony)
Black

MATERIALS

Brushes
- 5/0 script liner
- no. 2 round
- no. 2 flat

Additional Supplies
- DecoArt Multi-Purpose Sealer
- sanding oval or fine-grit sandpaper
- tracing paper
- pencil
- white or light graphite paper
- stylus
- DecoArt DuraClear Satin Varnish

Surface
- from Walnut Hollow

❧ This pattern may be hand-traced or photocopied for personal use only. It appears here at full size.

Roses and Lilacs

THIS SIMPLE ROSE design uses warm flowers against a cool background. Tiny fill flowers against the large roses create contrast, and subtle burnishes on the leaves create interest. The triadic combination of primary colors is used for this project.

PREPARATION

Base the entire surface with a brush mix of equal amounts of Blue/Grey Mist and Multi-Purpose Sealer using a foam brush. When dry, sand lightly and transfer the pattern with white or light graphite paper. With the large flat brush, float Blue Haze around the scallops. Load the liner with Buttermilk and paint the scallops.

ROSES

Base the roses with Raspberry using the rose angle brush. Add Burgundy Wine to the short side of the brush and blend on the palette. Make a U near the top of the rose, sliding down one side, patting across and sliding up the remaining side of the rose shape. Make a larger U farther down the rose to divide the flower into three equal parts.

Add Warm Neutral and a little Baby Pink to the long side of the dirty brush. Starting at the back half of the cup, paint upside-down U shapes to form the back part of individual petals. The side petals are done with these same colors blended on the palette.

Add Baby Pink and a little Titanium White to the long side of the brush and add a drop of blending gel. Wipe the brush lightly on a paper towel if it is too heavy with paint. Paint the fronts of the petals using the technique above.

Add more petals to fill out the flower, making the petals lighter as you work forward to the front and bottom of the rose.

FILL FLOWERS

Base the fill flowers with a brush mix of Blue Haze and a little Warm Neutral using the deerfoot brush. Add a little Titanium White to the dirty brush for the highlight. Fill the no. 8 flat with Blue Haze, edge with Warm Neutral and a little Titanium White and stroke the individual petals. For the centers, paint dots of Yellow Ochre and then a few of Raw Sienna.

LEAVES

Base the leaves with a brush mix of Warm Neutral and Avocado using the no. 12 flat. Shade first with Avocado and then add a final shading of Plantation Pine plus a little Burgundy Wine. With the small flat brush, add the calyx to the buds using these same colors. Burnish or add bug bites to a few of the leaves with a mix of Plantation Pine, Burgundy Wine and Raw Sienna. Side load this mix on the flat brush and float down the edges of the leaves.

Finish as described on page 26.

DecoArt Americana

| Titanium (Snow) White | Buttermilk | Yellow Ochre | Warm Neutral | Baby Pink | Blue/Grey Mist | Raspberry |

| Burgundy Wine | Raw Sienna | Blue Haze | Avocado | Plantation Pine |

MATERIALS

Brushes
- 5/0 script liner
- small deerfoot
- ⅜" (10mm) rose angle
- no. 8 flat
- no. 12 flat
- 1" (25mm) foam brush

Additional Supplies
- DecoArt Multi-Purpose Sealer
- sanding oval or fine-grit sandpaper
- tracing paper
- pencil
- white or light graphite paper
- stylus
- DecoArt Brush 'n Blend Extender
- DecoArt DuraClear Satin Varnish

Surface
- from Designs by Bentwood

❧ *This pattern may be hand-traced or photo-copied for personal use only. Enlarge at 164 percent to bring it up to full size.*

Container of Daisies

THIS DESIGN IS A triadic combination of yellow, red and blue. I used bottle colors instead of mixing each color myself. Sometimes I feel like mixing colors, and other times I just want to sit down and paint.

Notice that the flowers are twice the height of the container they're in—it's just that simple.

PREPARATION
Base the surface with a brush mix of Black Forest Green and Multi-Purpose Sealer. Transfer the pattern with white graphite paper and a stylus.

CONTAINER
Base the container with Marigold. Load the large flat with Marigold and edge into Raw Sienna. Keep the Raw Sienna to the outside edge and stroke toward the center. Add more Marigold and then edge into Light Buttermilk and apply in the center area. Dampen and float Burnt Sienna on the outside edges of the container. Dampen again and apply Light Buttermilk with the chisel edge of the brush in the center area. Add Marigold to the middle value area and Burnt Sienna near the edges. Blot and blend the chisel lines. Paint the top and bottom edges with the round filled with Marigold, shade and highlight as described above. Float a shadow of Lamp Black around the container to set it in the scene.

LEAVES
Load the flat with Avocado Green and edge one corner into Black Forest Green. Start at the stem end and paint one half of the leaf. Flip the brush and repeat on other side. Add more Black Forest Green as you work back into the design. Detail the leaves with floated Raw Sienna, Marigold plus just a little Avocado, Prussian Blue and Lamp Black.

FILL FLOWERS
Paint the center front fill flowers with a brush mix of Prussian Blue and a little Light Buttermilk, adding more Prussian Blue as you work back in the design. Float Prussian Blue to separate the petals. Highlight with a brush mix of Titanium White and a touch of Prussian Blue; outline the petals nearest the center of interest with this same mix. Mix Prussian Blue, Alizarin Crimson and a touch of Titanium White and paint small background flowers. Dab centers with Burnt Sienna and Olde Gold. Add a touch of Cadmium Yellow to the front flowers. Add stamen dots of Titanium White to the front flowers; use a brush mix of Lamp Black and Titanium White for a few, and only Lamp Black for the remaining stamen dots.

DAISIES
For the side daisies, stroke petals with Burnt Sienna, working wet-into-wet. Wipe brush, fill with Marigold and stroke between previous petals. Repeat with Light Buttermilk on the front half of the flower only. For the center daisies, use Olde Gold, Golden Straw and Titanium White. Dab the center of the main daisy with Burnt Sienna. Edge brush into a little Black Forest Green and pull around the center. Add a small circle of Cadmium Yellow dots in the center. Add stamen dots of Lamp Black, a few of Titanium White, and one of Black Forest Green in the middle. For remaining daisies, dab centers with Burnt Sienna plus a little Black Forest Green. Edge brush into Black Forest Green and pull around the center. Add a circle of Olde Gold dots and stamen dots of Lamp Black and a few of Light Buttermilk.

Finish as described on page 26.

DecoArt Americana

Titanium
(Snow) White

Light
Buttermilk

Cadmium
Yellow

Marigold

Golden Straw

Olde Gold

Raw Sienna

Burnt Sienna

Alizarin
Crimson

Avocado

Black Forest
Green

Prussian Blue

Lamp (Ebony)
Black

MATERIALS

Brushes
- 5/0 script
- no. 4 round
- no. 10 flat
- ¾" (19mm) flat

Additional Supplies
- DecoArt Multi-Purpose Sealer
- sanding oval or fine-grit sandpaper
- tracing paper
- pencil
- white graphite paper
- stylus
- DecoArt DuraClear Satin Varnish

Surface
- from Catalina Cottage

This pattern may be hand-traced or photocopied for personal use only. Enlarge at 133 percent to bring it up to full size.

THIS PROJECT PUTS to the test the theory about temperature affecting the perceived depth of an object. I've designed this piece to have different planes, each containing either warm, cool or in-between roses and leaves. This project uses the triadic combination of primary colors.

PREPARATION AND BACKGROUND
Base the lid with a brush mix of Green Mist and Multi-Purpose Sealer. Base the remainder of the box with a brush mix of Deep Teal and Multi-Purpose Sealer. Dampen the background with water. Brush mix one part Deep Teal and two parts glazing medium and apply to wet lid. Crumple a plastic bag and dab the surface to get a subtle background. Use this same technique with Antique Teal for the bottom. Allow to dry and then transfer the pattern. Float Forest Green around the leaves and flowers in the back half of the design; float Antique Teal around items in the front area.

LEAVES
Base the leaves with Forest Green. Shade the leaves with a brush mix of Forest Green and Black Forest Green, starting at the tip of the leaf and wiggling down. Highlight the warm leaves (those in the front of the design) with a brush mix of Forest Green and a bit of Olive Green. Mix Forest Green and Green Mist to highlight the cool leaves.

FILL FLOWERS
Base the warm fill flowers with a brush mix of Raw Sienna and a touch of Cadmium Yellow. Add Titanium White for the highlight strokes. Outline some of the petals with a mix of Titanium White and Cadmium Yellow.

Base the cool fill flowers with Raw Sienna. Add Titanium White to the dirty brush for the lightest areas and to outline some of the petals.

Base the centers of the warm flowers with Antique Teal and a little Alizarin Crimson. Add dots of Cadmium Yellow and a few dots each of Titanium White and Raw Sienna. Base the centers of the cool flowers with Antique Teal and a little Raw Sienna. Add dots using the same colors as for the warm centers.

ROSES AND BUDS
Base the warm roses and buds with Raspberry on the angle brush, adding Alizarin Crimson on the short side. Add Titanium White to the long side as needed. For the calyxes on the warm flowers, fill the no. 12 flat with Forest Green and pull Olive Green on one side of the

brush. Keep the light side up and stroke on the calyx.

Base the cool rose and buds with Antique Mauve on the angle brush, adding Napa Red on the short side. For the calyxes, fill the no. 12 flat and pull in Cadmium Yellow. Keep the light side up as you paint.

Load the liner with a mix of Raw Sienna, Black Forest Green and a touch of Alizarin Crimson and paint the vines.

Finish as described on page 26.

DecoArt Americana

 Titanium (Snow) White

 Cadmium Yellow

 Raw Sienna

 Raspberry

 Antique Mauve

 Alizarin Crimson

 Napa Red

 Olive Green

 Green Mist

 Deep Teal

 Forest Green

 Antique Teal

 Black Forest Green

MATERIALS

Brushes
- 5/0 script liner
- no. 2 filbert
- ⅜" (10mm) rose angle
- no. 4 flat
- ¾" (19mm) flat

Additional Supplies
- DecoArt Multi-Purpose Sealer
- DecoArt Faux Glaze Medium
- plastic shopping bag
- tracing paper
- pencil
- graphite paper
- stylus
- DecoArt DuraClear Satin Varnish

Surface
- from Catalina Cottage

❧ *This pattern may be hand-traced or photocopied for personal use only. Enlarge at 143 percent to bring it up to full size.*

Hindeloopen Birds

THE CENTER OF interest in this design is the birds. You can see that the tips of the wings and bellies of the birds get our attention first. I have used a darker border to help keep your eye pulled to the lighter areas in the design. This piece uses the split complementary colors of blue-green, orange and red.

PREPARATION
Base the surface with equal parts Antique Teal and Multi-Purpose Sealer. When dry, sand lightly and transfer pattern. Dampen the banding with water using a large flat brush. Load the wet brush with one part Midnite Blue and three parts glazing medium. Smoothly paint mixture around the edge, then dab with a crumpled plastic bag.

LEAVES
Base the leaves with strokes of Deep Teal. Add light strokes of Green Mist to some of the leaves. On the larger leaves, add linework with a brush mix of Buttermilk and Green Mist loaded on the script liner.

FLOWERS
Base the yellow flowers with Raw Sienna. Shade separately with Heritage Brick and Marigold. Add highlights of a brush mix of Buttermilk and a touch of Marigold.

Base the rusty red flowers with Gingerbread. Shade

separately with Heritage Brick and Peach Sherbet. Add linework with a brush mix of Buttermilk and a little Peach Sherbet loaded on the script liner.

Base the blue flowers with Blue Haze and shade separately with Midnight Blue and Blue Mist. Highlight with linework using a brush mix of Buttermilk and a touch of Blue Mist.

Paint the stems for stick flowers by filling the no. 2 round brush with Deep Teal and pulling in a little Green Mist. Paint the peach flowers with Heritage Brick and over-stroke with Gingerbread. The blue flowers are done the same way but with Midnite Blue and Blue Mist.

BIRDS
Base the body of the left-hand bird with Blue Haze, shade with Midnite Blue and highlight with Buttermilk. Base the tail with Raw Sienna and add Buttermilk, then Marigold. Add a little Gingerbread and then add Titanium White for highlight. Base the wing with Heritage Brick and add some middle-value feathers of Gingerbread. Highlight with Buttermilk. Paint the eye Midnite Blue and add linework of Buttermilk. Paint the bill with Raw Sienna.

Base the body of the bird on the right with Blue Mist and shade with Blue Haze. Use Buttermilk to add light strokes to the head and belly. Base the tail with Heritage Brick and highlight with Buttermilk. Base the wing with Raw Sienna and add light strokes of Buttermilk.

Base the body of the center bird with Midnite Blue and add light strokes of Blue Mist along the edge. Base the wing with Blue Haze and shade with Midnite Blue. Edge Blue Mist on the wing tips and pull toward the body. Add Buttermilk for the final light value on the front wing. Base the tail with Heritage Brick and edge with Gingerbread. Add a few strokes each of Raw Sienna and Buttermilk.

Finish as described on page 26.

DecoArt Americana

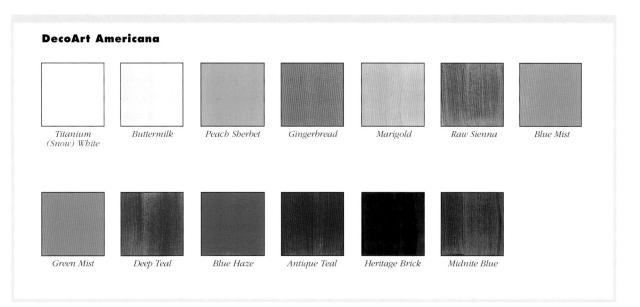

Titanium (Snow) White	*Buttermilk*	*Peach Sherbet*	*Gingerbread*	*Marigold*	*Raw Sienna*	*Blue Mist*

Green Mist	*Deep Teal*	*Blue Haze*	*Antique Teal*	*Heritage Brick*	*Midnite Blue*

MATERIALS

Brushes
- 5/0 script liner
- no. 2 round
- no. 4 round
- ¾" (19mm) flat

Additional Supplies
- DecoArt Multi-Purpose Sealer
- sanding oval or fine-grit sandpaper
- DecoArt Faux Glaze Medium
- plastic shopping bag
- tracing paper
- pencil
- graphite paper
- stylus
- DecoArt DuraClear Satin Varnish

Surface
- from Catalina Cottage

This pattern may be hand-traced or photo-copied for personal use only. Enlarge at 154 percent to bring it up to full size.

COLOR CONVERSION CHART

DecoArt Americana	Delta Ceramcoat	Jo Sonja Artists	Plaid FolkArt
Admiral Blue	Prussian Blue + Purple	Storm Blue + Pacific Blue + Diox Purple (2:1:1)	
Alizarin Crimson	Berry Red	Permanent Alizarine + Burnt Umber	Holiday Red
Antique Mauve	Dusty Mauve	Plum Pink + Purple Madder (1:T)	Rose Garden
Antique Teal	Blue Spruce	Teal + Colony Blue (2:1)	
Antique White	Trail Tan + White	Smoked Pearl + Raw Sienna (2:1)	Linen
Arbor Green	Green Sea + Alpine Green (1:T)	Green Oxide + Antique Green	
Asphaltum	Walnut + Burnt Umber	Raw Umber	
Avocado	Forest Green	Pine Green + Antique Green + Carbon Black (2:1:T)	Clover
Baby Pink	Rose Petal Pink + Fuschia (2:1)	Titanium White + Napthol Crimson + Brilliant Magenta (1:T:T)	Baby Pink
Berry Red	Napthol Crimson	Brown Madder + Napthol Crimson (2:1)	Engine Red
Black Forest Green	Hunter Green	Pthalo Green + Carbon Black (1:T)	Wintergreen
Black Green	Black Green		Wrought Iron
Black Plum	Chocolate Cherry	Diox Purple + Indian Red Oxide + Burnt Umber	Burnt Carmine
Blue Grey Mist	Blue Mist + Adriatic Blue	Nimbus Grey + Antique Green + French Blue (2:1:1)	
Blue Haze	Blue Spruce + Avalon Blue	Storm Blue + Nimbus Grey (2:1)	Township Blue
Blue Mist	Blue Wisp	Nimbus Grey + Celadon + Antique Green (2:1:1)	Teal Blue
Blue Violet	Ultra Blue	Ultra Blue Deep + Amethyst (4:1)	
Burgundy Wine	Black Cherry	Indian Red Oxide + Brown Madder + Brown Earth (3:2:1)	Burgundy
Burnt Sienna	Candy Bar Brown + Burgundy Rose	Burnt Sienna	Burnt Sienna
Buttermilk	Butter Cream	Warm White + Raw Sienna (1:T)	
Cadmium Red	Fruit Punch	Napthol Red Light	Light Red
Cadmium Yellow	Bright Yellow + Crocus	Cadmium Yellow Mid + Indian Yellow (2:1)	Sunny Yellow
Camel	Maple Sugar Tan	Naples Yellow Hue + Raw Sienna	
Celery Green	Stonewedge Green + Sea Grass (1:T)	Olive Green + Smoked Pearl (2:1)	
Cherry Red	Bright Red	Napthol Crimson + Permanent Alizarine (2:1)	Lipstick Red
Cool Neutral	Sandstone + Stonewedge Green (1:T)	Smoked Pearl + Provincial Beige + Antique Green (2:1:T)	
Country Blue	Periwinkle Blue	Pacific Blue + Unbleached Titanium	Light Periwinkle
Dark Pine	Hunter Green + Alpine Green (1:T)	Pthalo Green + Teal + Brilliant Green (2:2:1)	
Deep Burgundy	Barn Red	Indian Red Oxide + Permanent Alizarine	Alizarin Crimson
Deep Teal	Woodland Night Green	Teal + Jade (2:1)	Tartan Green
Desert Sand	Sandstone + Trail Tan	Smoked Pearl + Raw Sienna+ Sap Green (2:1:T)	Clay Bisque
Dioxazine Purple	Purple	Dioxazine Purple	Dioxazine Purple
Evergreen	Dark Jungle Green	Hookers Green + Carbon Black (1:T)	Olive Green
Forest Green	Dark Foliage Green	Hookers Green + Jade (2:1)	Green Meadow
Gingerbread	Caucasian Flesh + Poppy Orange (1:T)	Gold Oxide + Rose Pink + Opal (2:1:1)	

**** Mix equal portions of colors unless otherwise noted. T denotes just a touch of color.*

DecoArt Americana	Delta Ceramcoat	Jo Sonja Artists	Plaid FolkArt
Golden Straw	Straw	Turners Yellow + Naples Yellow Hue + Raw Sienna	Buttercup
Green Mist	Alpine Green + White (1:T)	Jade + Antique Green (2:1)	Poetry Green
Heritage Brick	Red Iron Oxide + Burgundy Rose	Purple Madder + Burnt Sienna	
Jade Green	Wedgewood Green	Pine Green + Smoked Pearl	Bayberry
Lamp (Ebony) Black	Black	Carbon Black	Ivory Black
Lt. Avocado	English Yew Green + Wedgewood Green	Olive Green + Nimbus Grey + Burnt Umber	
Light Buttermik	Light Ivory	Warm White + Naples Yellow Hue (3:1)	Warm White
Marigold	Empire Gold	Turners Yellow + Yellow Oxide (2:1)	
Midnite Blue	Manganese	Prussian Blue + Carbon Black (1:T)	Thunder Blue
Moon Yellow	Old Parchment + Crocus Yellow (2:1)	Turners Yellow + Naples Yellow Hue	Buttercrunch
Napa Red	Barn Red + Maroon	Burgundy + Burnt Umber (2:1)	Berry Wine
Napthol Red	Bright Red	Napthol Red Light + Napthol Crimson (2:1)	Christmas Red
Neutral Grey	Hippo Grey + Lichen Grey (2:1)	Nimbus Grey + Provincial Beige + Carbon Black + Burnt Umber (1:1:T:T)	Medium Grey
Olde Gold	Mustard	Moss Green + Yellow Oxide	
Olive Green	Green + Leaf Green (2:1)	Green Light + Smoked Pearl (2:1)	
Orchid	Lilac + Lilac Dusk (1:T)	Amethyst + Warm White (2:1)	Orchid
Peach Sherbet	Coral + Rosetta Pink	Jaune Brilliant + Gold Oxide	
Plantation Pine	Gamal Green	Hookers Green + Burnt Umber (2:1)	Southern Pine
Primary Blue	Opaque Blue	Paynes Grey + Pthalo Blue (2:1)	True Blue
Primary Red	Opaque Red	Permanent Alizarine + Napthol Crimson (2:1)	Calico Red
Primary Yellow	Yellow	Yellow Deep	School Bus Yellow
Prussian Blue	Navy Blue + Blueberry (2:1)	Prussian Blue + Paynes Grey + Ultra Deep Blue (1:2:1)	Prussian Blue
Raspberry Pink	Wild Rose	Plum Pink + Rose Pink (2:1)	Raspberry Sherbet
Raw Sienna	Raw Sienna	Burnt Sienna + Raw Sienna + Provincial Beige	Raw Sienna
Red Violet	Sweetheart Blush + Magenta	Red Violet	Fuchsia
Royal Purple	Vintage Wine + Dusty Plum	Brilliant Violet + Diox Purple + Carbon Black (1:1:T)	
Sand	Antique White	Warm White + Yellow Oxide + Raw Sienna (1:T:T)	Taffy
Santa Red	Opaque Red	Permanent Alizarine + Napthol Crimson	Napthol Crimson
Slate Grey	Drizzle Grey + Black (1:T)	Titanium White + Carbon Black (4:1)	
Tangelo Orange	Tangerine	Vermillion	Autumn Leaves
Tangerine	Yellow + Bittersweet Orange	Indian Yellow + Cadmium Orange + Jaune Brilliant (1:T:T)	
Titanium (Snow) White	White	Titanium White	White (Titanium)
True Ochre	Antique Gold	Yellow Oxide + Raw Sienna	Yellow Ochre
Violet Haze	Purple Dusk	Brilliant Violet + French Blue + Smoked Pearl (2:1:1)	Grey Plum
Viridian Green	Phthalo Green	Pthalo Green + Prussian Blue Hue (2:T)	Pthalo Green
Warm Neutral	Wild Rice + Misty Mauve	Fawn + Skin Tone Base	Milkshake
Yellow Light	Bright Yellow	Yellow Light	Yellow Light
Yellow Ochre	Cloudberry Tan + White	Raw Sienna + Naples Yellow Hue + Moss Green (2:1:T)	

INDEX